Where Have All The Fathers Gone?

Daily Thoughts for Dads, Dads-To-Be & Papas

JOE GROTE

Where Have All the Fathers Gone?
JOE GROTE

Printed in the United States of America
First edition

ISBN 979-8-9890968-0-0

Cover and interior designed by Stephen Sullivan
Cover illustration by Tom Miller
Interior illustration by John Kitzmiller

FROM

TO

To my wife Ann,
For teaching me what love is.

INTRODUCTION

There is no perfect family. Fathers come in all shapes and sizes. No two families are the same. You may, for way too many reasons to count, not live with your child/children daily. Even more reason to let them know how much you love them. Poor examples of fathers who don't live with their children are all around us. The best examples follow the same action described above. They love their kids. They treat others with respect. They are responsible for their actions. These men deserve even more credit for accepting their call to be father to their children.

When I was child, there was a popular song entitled: "Where Have All the Flowers Gone?" These days, it seems like we could change the wording to: "Where Have All the Fathers Gone?" The evidence is all around us. The percentage of incarcerated men in our country that didn't have a father in their life is over 80%. The percentage of teenagers who are "hardcore" drug users is over 90%. If you polled teachers throughout the country, they would tell you that children without fathers make up the highest percentage of high school dropouts. The list could go on and on. Sadly, there is no single solution to the problem. Seemingly, the simple recognition that there is a problem would be enough. So why do the stats keep growing?

Okay, so enough of the bad news. What can you do about it? If you are reading these daily thoughts, you are most likely going to be a father, you are a father or you are a grandfather. Maybe the first step is to start in your own home. Grab onto the responsibility of raising your children/grandchildren so that they do not add to the negative statistics. Start by telling them you love them. Love their mother. Treat all those you meet with respect. Be responsible for your actions.

You may notice that I have taken the liberty to use the first person in writing some of these passages. My own walk as a father has had its ups and downs just like yours. It is my hope that my insights are informative and hopefully somewhat inspirational as well. Being a Catholic Deacon, some of the daily selections may "lean" toward Catholic teachings. However, these selections have a universal message. I hope you will indulge me for adding them to the Christian walk which pervades the themes expressed throughout.

The pages you are going to be reading are intended to help make you more aware of how love starts in your relationship with those you call your own. By accepting that responsibility, you may find yourself following a path of success for not only your children and their mother, but ultimately for yourself as well. Happy kids come from happy moms and dads. Happy kids aren't burdened with fear. Happy kids lead healthy and meaningful lives.

Regardless of when you start reading this book, start on the calendar date you receive it. Don't read ahead. Don't look at what came before. This is not a book to be consumed in a few days, a week or even a month. It is a collection to be read daily and to be reflected upon. I encourage you to make it a part of your daily life. I pray that you find hope, guidance and most of all, a greater sense of the love that will pervade your life by accepting your call to be the father your child/children deserve.

"It is well with my soul, for I have learned to be content whatever the circumstances."

– PHILLIPIANS 4:11

January 1

THE SOLEMNITY OF MARY

On this day, we acknowledge that Mary was indeed the MOTHER OF GOD.

Mary was the mother of Jesus, who was both human and divine.

It is a mystery of Christian faith that a human could be and was, the Mother of God.

What a gift and what a challenge it was for Mary to accept this responsibility.

Would I be willing to accept such a gift?

Do you know anyone who would?

Today, take time to celebrate the divine and virginal motherhood of the blessed virgin.

"And Mary kept all these things, reflecting on them in her heart."

– Luke 2:19

Did you tell your wife you love her today?

January 2
RESOLUTIONS

Many of us are challenged during this time of year to make resolutions.

Most of which we either forget or break before the month of January is over.

What may be in order, instead, is to look at our daily habits.

What do you do daily that is frivolous?

What or who do you leave out because of your habits?

What do you do that is selfish?

Each of us has a wish to do more for ourselves, our families, our friends.

What can you do each day to make more time for yourself

so that you can be a better husband, father or friend?

Don't beat yourself up over this.

The challenge is to acknowledge what you do that keeps you from being who you want to be.

Whose day did you "make" today?

January 3
WHO ARE YOUR FRIENDS?

"Remember George: No man is a failure who has friends."

Coming out of the Christmas Season, it may seem trite to refer to a line from "It's a Wonderful Life," however, it fits perfectly as we look into counting our blessings. For some of us, we spend a lot more time with our friends than our family. The reasons for this are many. However, in today's world of digital communication, a man with one or two close friends is considered a lucky man. How many close friends can you count? If it is more than two, get down on your knees and thank the Lord. Also, be happy that God has placed these people in your life. Think about how dreary your life would be without them.

Also, you have had a hand in forming these relationships over the years. Good for you!

Now, pray that others around you are just as fortunate.

Did you call or text a friend a message of hope today?

January 4
ACCEPT THE POSITION

You don't become a great dad overnight. Okay, admit it. It takes time. If your children are younger, sure, you get a smile or a laugh from infants and toddlers. Then, they grow up and the daily chances to interact with them become fewer and fewer. Being there to help with homework, reading with them and/or praying at bedtime provide opportunities for memories that they may not recall until years later.

But, be there. It's the times that you are not there, even on the normal days, opportunities for memories are lost. It's a sacrifice with untold rewards. They will be grateful as they grow up and hear stories from other kids about their absent father. Don't be one of the dads that is absent. It's often a thankless position to be in. But accept the position. You have the credentials. Your reward will be great in heaven.

Did you tell your kids you love them today?

January 5

A FATHER'S LETTER TO HIS CHILD

LIFE IS NOT PERFECT. No matter how much we want it to be, life is not perfect. You are perfect. I can say that because I am your father. I know your heart. But, no matter how much I want your life to be perfect, I know it is not going to be. Sometimes, life is messy. I cannot live your life, I can only pray that God is with you, every moment of every day. I must realize my role is to want the best for you. But I know that every life comes up short of the perfection we want for each other.

So, we live each day as He wills it, knowing our will always falls short of His. And yet, we persevere. So, I will watch as your life unfolds, hoping and praying for the best, knowing that life doesn't always work out that way. That is why we must have each other to hug, to share our sorrows and to celebrate our successes. Getting down on our knees in sorrow and success, Knowing that we have grown through both.

Did you tell your kids you love them today?

January 6
EPIPHANY

Do you still have any sign of the Christmas season around your home? Most of us have already taken our tree and decorations down. Our minds have turned to paying bills and wondering about filing our taxes. The season of Christmas doesn't officially end until today. Have we so quickly turned our thoughts to the natural instead of continuing to revel in the supernatural? Our Lord has come! The Magi came to "do Him homage." Can't we at least try to do the same?

Here is an easy way to keep a sign of the season up from the beginning until the end of the season. Put up your manger crèche on Thanksgiving weekend and keep it up through at least today.

"We saw His star at its rising, and have come to do Him homage."
– Matthew 2:2

Say a prayer of gratitude today for one of the blessings in your life.

January 7

BE ON THE JOB

We have all heard stories about fathers who are absent or never involved in their children's lives. Fathers who always have an excuse to be somewhere else than with their family. Do they just not care, or do they just not know how to be a father? Becoming a dad doesn't happen today or tomorrow. You don't become a dad overnight. There are no manuals to read to show us how. We all receive on the job training for this position. But that is the key.

We must be "on the job." Simply being present is the first step. Your daily interactions with your wife and children provide opportunities for growth. We grow even on the most normal days. Which if you think about it, is just about every day. What foundation have you built for the rough days? Praying for and with your family is the start of a good foundation.

Ask St. Joseph to help provide this foundation. Look what he did for his Son in the "normal" days.

Did you tell your kids you love them today?

January 8
BAPTISM OF OUR LORD

John the Baptist came to proclaim that "one that was mightier than he was coming." He was largely ignored. However, a few of his followers would become apostles. In the New Testament we see Jesus coming to John to be baptized. John at first wished to be baptized by Jesus, but fulfilled what was prophesied. Soon after, we hear John is arrested and eventually put to death because of Herod's promise to the teenage daughter of his illegitimate wife.

Both John and Jesus fulfilled their baptism mission. What is your mission? How are you working to fulfill it.

"And a voice came from the heavens, saying, 'This is my beloved Son, in whom I am well pleased.'"
– Matthew 3:17

Did you call or text a message of hope today?

January 9

HAVE YOUR HOME BLESSED

It doesn't cost you anything and the blessings can be eternal. Have your home blessed. Ask your pastor, or deacon or minister to come to your home and make it truly a holy place. You won't notice a physical difference, but there will be an invisible difference. The devil hates the presence of God. Holy water is your defense against the devil. Use all the defense you can get in the battle against evil. You may even develop a closer relationship with your pastor, deacon or minister. Talk about a heavenly reward!

Whose day did you make today?

January 10
THE CONCEPT OF TIME

If you believe in an afterlife, it is said that it is timeless. There is only a perpetual NOW in heaven. We are so preoccupied in our lives that sometimes we truly forget to "live" our lives. What if you could bring that sense of timelessness into your home. Watch your children closely. They have little sense of time. It is not until we impose time on them that they begin to react to it. Here is a suggestion. Have a timeless Saturday morning. Put your phone away. Take off your watch if you have one. Sit on the floor with your children and play with them. Forget about time and they will too. Then watch your level of joy grow. They have it right in heaven. Bring it home.

Did you tell your kids you love them today?

January 11

HAVE DREAMS

Dreams are different than plans. Dreams are life longing for itself. You are made for greater things. Dream big. Share your dreams and watch them take even greater importance to not only you but your wife and family. Be patient. Be realistic. "Rome wasn't built in a day." Some of the greatest achievements in human history were completed when the dreamer was seventy, eighty or ninety years old. So, do you think you don't have time to fulfill your dreams? Think again.

Whose day did you "make" today?

January 12
ETERNAL PATIENCE

Who do you think is more patient? The battle for souls has been going on since Adam and Eve were in the garden. There is no way to know how long the fallen angels had been competing with God when He decided to create us in His image. The devil grasped the opportunity to test our free will and he scored a victory. A victory that we have been paying for ever since. Over the millennia since the fall, the battle for our souls has ebbed and flowed. It seems obvious that lately the flow is leaning to the devil's side. But even the devil knows that in the end, he cannot win. So, each of us must decide whose patience we want to test. Test the devil's patience, side with his enemy.

Who did you pray for today?

January 13

FIND A MENTOR

There isn't a man among us who doesn't need a mentor once in a while. Mentors can help with so many things. Little things like knowledge about cars, or how to improve your golf swing, or how to grow a garden. Then, there are mentors who help with the big things: Your relationship with your wife, your faith life, unexpected health problems. Don't be so impressed with yourself that you don't look for help when you need it, because, you are usually the last one to know you need help. Others will see it in you. Prove them right. Ask for help.

Whose day did you "make" today?

January 14
BE A MENTOR

What are you passionate about? What is it that you make sure you have time to do? Whatever it is, that should be your mantra. Every mentor has one. Know what your gifts are and freely make them available to those you encounter along the way. You are better at something than most people you know. If you aren't sure what your gift is, then ask your closest friend. Don't get a big head. It's a gift, share it.

Whose day did you "make" today?

January 15

EXERCISE

Have you seen them? You know, the commercials that bombard us this time of year to lose weight and exercise. As if the rest of the year we can forget that we need to do it as well. Of course, physical exercise is necessary, but how do we find time for it?

The type of exercise we all need is mental. If we can get our mind to "put its arms around our needs," then the physical part is easier. Maybe we can start by focusing on our faith. Then, we can see the order and priority of our daily lives. Do we spend much time each day in prayer? Do you even acknowledge God before noon, or even at dinner?

Maybe you can make a mental note to start each day with a prayer of thanksgiving for the gift of another day. Then ask yourself. What are your needs? What are your priorities?

Did you tell your kids you love them today?

January 16

KNOW WHEN TO TAKE A STAND

Dr. Martin Luther King dedicated his entire life to bringing awareness to the plight of black Americans. Whether you agree with his methods or not, his dedication was unmistakable. The change that he and the movement he fostered brought to countless lives is immeasurable. Heroes like Dr. King and Rosa Parks stood up when others were afraid. Such leaders come along once in a generation. Sometimes even less often than that.

Being head of a family brings great responsibility. Your wife and children need your leadership.

What do you stand for? Are you the leader in your family? Do you take a stand when called to?

Whose day did you "make" today?

January 17

DO YOU HAVE PLANS?

It is in most people's human nature to plan for the future. How is your plan going? Not seeing the results you expected? With whom did you consult while you were making your plans? Life is what happens while you make plans. Be flexible. Be patient. Make sure your plans are His plans. Plan together with your wife. If she buys into your plans, you will have much greater happiness and success. You are not in this alone

---

Did you tell your wife you love her today?

January 18

BE MORE LIKE JESUS, TOMORROW

He probably never owned more than one tunic. He slept wherever he ended up at the end of the day. He never traveled more than forty miles from where he was born. He sought out sinners, the poor and the outcast. And yet, he has influenced more people across the world than anyone who has ever lived. How? He lived the Truth. He told us to love our neighbor as ourselves. Admit it. You have a hard time living up to that. Here's the good part. You just have to try to be better tomorrow. Maybe that's something you can paste on your mirror.

"Try to be better tomorrow." One day at a time.

Whose day did you "make" today?

January 19

TEACH RESPECT OF THE HUMAN BODY

Due to the influence of social media, we are less and less in real human contact than in the past. We are not sure how to connect with each other one-on-one. Has this led to less and less respect for each other and maybe even ourselves? Teach your children to start by respecting their own human body. Show them respect by treating your wife like the gift she is. If they don't know about this respect, they will not know how to act with those they encounter in school and other social situations. Teach them that their body is a temple to be respected and that those they encounter deserve the same respect. Respect can be taught. Respect is earned. Be sure your children are well taught.

Did you tell your kids you love them today?

January 20

IT'S A WAR WORTH FIGHTING

There is a war going on that many recognize, but few are doing much about it. It is a war that crept into our world somewhat sheepishly, but now is pervading most of society. It is a war on the nuclear family. Few in the media wish to acknowledge it and even fewer are willing to put up money to help stop it. You know why? There is little monetary profit in it. But the loss is infinitely greater than any monetary value you could place on it. The cost in human lives lost to broken families is infinite. The battle must be fought. Which side of the battle are you on? As in most all battles, we choose sides at our own peril.

Did you tell your kids you love them today?

January 21
RUSH TO JUDGEMENT

We are inundated with story after story in the 24-hour news cycle that points to "the other side" as the culprit for society's ills. This technique works because it identifies a 'so-called' victim before true judgement can take place. News directors need content. They want to be first with the story, sometimes ignoring whether the story is correct or not. This type of judgement has permeated our everyday lives. People's lives can be ruined because we rush to judgement. Don't let the "need to know" get in the way of finding the truth.

Did you call or text a friend a message of hope today?

January 22

PRAY FOR THE UNBORN

To the majority of us legal abortion is unthinkable. Today and around the world, we pray that the hearts and minds of those involved in abortion clinics and those fighting for abortion rights will look deep into their souls and realize what they are doing. We need to forget about why they think the way they do and appeal to their hearts. It is only through a change of heart that progress will be made. In fact, please consider making this part of your daily prayer routine. Pray that the hearts of those who support abortion will have a change of heart. Ask your wife and children to pray with you. And thank God that you have them with you to pray.

Did you tell your wife you love her today?

January 23

TEACH LIFE'S GREATEST LESSON

One of the mysteries of mankind is how, over the centuries, we have come to accept truly immoral laws. Think about abortion, euthanasia, selling of fetal tissue and cloning to name a few. Consider how it is possible that in human minds any of the above can be considered acceptable. What it comes down to is the realization that we cannot legislate morality. So how do we take a stand? Do it hand in hand. Take time to pray with your children and help them appreciate the gift of human life. Teach them to be selfless and to love life in all its forms. Teach them that love conquers all.

Did you tell your kids you love them today?

January 24
PRO GIFT

One of the most selfish acts a person can do is to abort a gift from God. That's right, a gift! Life is created when a man and woman engage in the most physically and mentally erotic act known to humankind. There is no greater pleasure than the gift of sexual union. And, the result of that greatest of feelings is completed when a baby is conceived. And what happens when someone refuses the gift and instead chooses an abortion, is a rejection of life's greatest gift. You lose out on the gift. What a slap in the face of Our Creator. Be Pro-Gift. Teach your children to be Pro-Gift. Shedding light on this greatest gift may help someone contemplating an abortion to rethink their decision. Thereby turning the most selfish of human acts into the most selfless. Accept the miracle of creation. Be Pro Gift, not Pro Choice.

Whose day did you "make" today?

January 25

THE CONVERSION OF ST. PAUL

He went around persecuting those who did not believe the way he did. He even took their lives in the name of his religion. Then one day, he was knocked off his horse and blinded by God. God asked, "Why do you persecute me?" Paul, as we know, was converted. He became not only a follower, but one of the leaders of the church he formally persecuted. His writings became part of our New Testament. He showed others the path to God and some of their writings became part of the New Testament. Not bad for a convert.

Did you call or text a friend a message of hope today?

January 26
WE HAVE LOST OUR SENSE OF MORALITY

When will it occur to society that our lost sense of morality is directly related to the ongoing demise of the nuclear family. It is not just the author's opinion. For decades, the loss of morality goes hand-in-hand with the loss of a father and mother living together under the same roof. Thankfully, some children whose parents don't live together still receive moral guidance from each parent. If kids don't find moral teaching in their homes, they will be left to find their own sense of morality from those they come into contact with. We used to be able to rely on schools to enhance the morality taught at home, and we can debate this all day long, but morality is a parent's responsibility. It should be strengthened in schools. It seems that now, this picture has been turned around. Parents, it's time you stood up and fought for the moral teaching that comes from loving parents. A good start is telling your children you love them. That's the start of good moral teaching

---

Did you tell your kids you love them today?

January 27
ST. THOMAS AQUINAS

He was or may still be your patron saint. He is the patron saint of students. And since our lives are a life-long journey for truth, we are all students. Thomas was actually imprisoned by his family because he wished to become a Dominican priest. Finally, they relented and allowed him to begin his studies. One of his greatest gifts to our faith is the work he did to show the grace that we receive through the sacraments. We honor him by regular reception of the sacraments. If someone asks you about your faith and you have a hard time giving them an answer, try Thomas':

"To one who has faith, no explanation is necessary. To one without faith, no explanation is possible."

Whose day did you "make" today?

January 28
HE EXISTS

He will lie to you at every turn. He will tell you that you are better than the guy at the desk behind you. He will convince you that flirting with the girl at the end of the bar is harmless. Try telling that to your wife. He will convince you that you deserve more money at work or more attention from you wife. He is the king of lies. The greatest one he inflicts us with is that he doesn't exist. Face it, he exists. He wants to bring you down. Don't listen. Don't acknowledge his countless lies. You will have a devil of a time getting out of the circumstances he wants to lead you into. Call him Satan, or the devil or Beelzebub. Whatever you call him, make it a collect call and hang up. He exists, don't encourage him.

Whose day did you "make" today?

January 29

ELIMINATE THE NEED

In repeated instances throughout history, man has tried to deal with problems with an ounce of precaution or throwing his hands up and saying there is nothing that can be done. Let's try the former way. An effective way to deal with a problem is to eliminate the need for it in the first place. Could this be an effective way to deal with abortion? Parents need to start at a young age, teaching their children the beauty of life and positive sex education that teaches that the human body is a temple that must be treasured. Here is a radical idea: Making this kind of education mandatory in all schools. It doesn't eliminate any one's rights. In fact, it would enhance them. What harm can come from at least trying? Parental involvement in teaching about the respect due each human body would be a great start. Why not start in your home?

Whose day did you "make" today?

January 30
YOUR BODY IS A TEMPLE

From their earliest childhood, your children need to hear you tell them that their body is a temple. Temples are not to be defiled. If they hear it starting at a young age, both boys and girls will learn to respect their own body and then as they grow older, they will respect those that they encounter as well. Mothers can also be bearers of this message. At an increasingly younger age, your children will be encouraged to "follow the crowd" and experiment with sexual ideas. By learning at a young age that their body is a temple, they will hopefully be prepared to reject the pressure and save themselves for intimate relations with their future spouse. Sound old-fashioned? Most of the best ideas are.

Did you tell your kids you love them today?

January 31
A TEXT WON'T DO

Our communication as a human race has taken an ugly turn. We think that because we can immediately text someone, we are communicating. Nothing takes the place of real human interaction. Countless studies show us that the more impersonal communication we utilize, the less connected we actually are. It is too easy to hide behind a texted response. I have news for you. Your wife, your children, your co-workers and those you worship with are longing for meaningful human interaction. Put down your phone. Use your God giving talent to be part of the lives of those around you.

Whose day did you "make" today?

"Do not neglect to show hospitality to strangers, for thereby some have entertained angels."

– HEBREWS 13:2

February 1

YOUR HOME IS A GIFT, SHARE IT

Do you have a roof over your head? If your answer is yes, whether you are renting or you own your home, you are better off than a large portion of the world. There are some who live not far from you who cannot say that. There are millions around the world who cannot say that. Share your home. Start with family. Then invite friends and/or neighbors. Opening your home seems to be a rare event these days. It's too much work, some will say. I don't have time, is another favorite reason. Stop with the excuses. Our world needs more human connection. What better way to engage with others than in the comfort of your own home. Remember, you could be entertaining angels. What have you got to lose?

Whose day did you "make" today?

February 2

IT'S GROUNDHOG DAY

Forget about the silly rodent in Pennsylvania. This day has come to symbolize being caught in a rut. Do you ever feel like you are in a rut? Does your faith need a little boost? Why not use today as the day to make a change. Suggest to your wife that you would like to pray with her. Or, better yet, gather the family around and say a prayer together. Ask each child to suggest someone or something for which they wish to pray. Soon, the rut may not seem so deep and with a little luck, maybe you will develop a new habit that will enhance the faith of your entire family.

Did you tell your kids you love them today?

February 3

TAKE CARE OF YOURSELF

Don't allow this to be a guilt trip. How are you feeling lately? Physically? Mentally? What should you do? Are your pants tighter? Could you jog 40 yards if you had to? Feeling bloated? If you aren't feeling better about yourself today than you did six months ago, maybe you have some work to do. No one is going to take care of you physically but you. Maybe your wife can help you eat a little better, but you have to put the fork down. If you have responsibility beyond yourself; you know what I mean: a wife, kids, parents who depend or will depend on you, maybe it's time to make some subtle changes. Make them subtle because big changes are hard to do. Start small. You will feel better mentally right away. The physical part will take a little longer

---

Say a prayer today for one of the blessings in your life.

February 4

EVERY HUMAN BEING IS FLAWED

Don't hold any human in such high esteem that you would be devastated if you found out they were not perfect. There has only ever been one perfect human being and He was crucified. Yes, He should be held in high esteem, but place your trust carefully. Keeping secrets is not something many of your fellow human beings can be trusted with. Confide only in a handful of close family and/or friends. To be human is to be flawed. Couch your expectations accordingly.

Did you call or text a friend a message of hope today?

February 5
BE THERE

Depending on how old your children are and how many you have, you have ample daily opportunities to give thanks to God. That should be enough said. But, did you pray for and/or with your children today? Do they know how much you love them? In today's world, even families are feeling less connected to each other physically and emotionally. There is no replacement for a hug, or a laugh, or a word of encouragement. Take time to be involved in the daily lives of your children so that they will have vivid memories of being loved and cherished. Then, just wait to see not only how they will become fathers and mothers like you without even knowing they are doing it. They will also be members of society that you wished they would become. "Be there" for your children. They will grow up to "be there" for you.

Did you tell your kids you love them today?

February 6

REMEMBER BEING A KID?

No matter how old you are, you will never lose the memory of your childhood years. Guess what, your children will not forget theirs either. You have the singular responsibility to make their childhood memories special. Don't put it off another day. Soon, your children will be grown and gone. Make memories today that will last a lifetime. Yours and theirs.

Did you tell your kids you love them today?

February 7

DON'T BE A STATISTIC

One stat you will never read about is: It is better for a child to grow up without a mother or a father. And yet, the stats grow with each passing day. There is no culture or society on earth that has thrived where fathers and/or mothers are not involved in the lives of their children. There is not a religion: Catholic, Muslim, Jewish, Protestant, Hindu, etc., that proports to downplay the crucial role of a father or mother in the family unit. And yet, with each passing day, there are more children born out of wedlock. Don't be a statistic, be a father. There is no reward for the former. Celebrate the latter.

Did you tell your wife you love her today?

February 8

WHAT DO YOU HAVE TO BE THANKFUL FOR?

How often do you thank those around you who have made a difference in your life? It is so easy to take for granted all those who have made an impact in our lives. Some, maybe by chance encounter, but in most cases, we have been formed over the years by those who love us. You may have even wondered why those you may have impacted in some way have yet to thank you. Have you thanked those that have impacted your life? Recall the ten lepers who were cured by Jesus and yet only one came back to thank him. Count your blessings. Take stock of those in your life who have formed you. And give thanks for them.

Say a prayer today for one of the blessings in your life.

February 9

YOU DESERVE RESPECT

They say respect is earned. But it is also taught. Children will learn respect at a young age. You cannot demand respect. It is learned over time and then applied to life's situations. Children can also be misled if they are around other kids whose parents haven't either taught or earned respect from their children. Be aware of subtle changes to your children's behavior if they are exposed to situations where parents have lost control of their own children. Explain to them that the behaviors they have seen elsewhere are not accepted in your home. You deserve respect. Teach it and earn it.

Did you tell your kids you love them today?

February 10

INDIVIDUAL SIGNIFICANCE

Now that I am ordained, I notice a sense of trust or added respect from others when I encounter them. A sense that what I say has more of a magnified importance. That is a lot of pressure to put on anyone. I would hope that each of us has this sense about those we encounter, regardless of our personal religious beliefs. A trust born out of each individual experience, unique in its own right and no less important. An individual significance born out of a walk that only they have lived.

Did you call or text a friend a message of hope today?

February 11
THAT AWFUL DISGUISE

No matter where you work, you will encounter people from all walks of life. Some of them you will befriend, some you will have casual discussions with and some will remain anonymous to you. Depending on the size of the workforce where you are, you may only develop relationships with a select few. And, of course, there are always some that you really try to avoid. The next time you have to deal with some you would rather avoid, remember the words of Mother Teresa. Whenever she had to deal with someone that she would rather avoid she would tell her sisters, "Here comes Jesus in that terrible disguise again." Offer it up. Maybe one day you will see a small opening that will lead to a better understanding of the plight of those you previously avoided.

Did you call or text a message of hope today?

February 12

WHAT A GIFT

Your wife is a gift, treat her that way. Little signs of appreciation go a long way. Daily "I love yous" are a start. A kiss on the check or a touch of your feet to hers when you go to bed at night are subtle reminders of the gift she is. Surprise her once in a while with flowers or make a dinner for her. Make sure your kids see you joking with her or sharing a sweet memory. Your relationship will last a lifetime. Your knowledge of the gift she is in your life need not be a distant memory. Make memories by intermittent affection. Believe me, your wife will remember when you do even the smallest thing to show affection. It's not how much you spend, it's how often you show her you care.

Did you tell your wife you love her today?

February 13

DATE NIGHT

When was the last time you had a date with your wife? I am not talking about New Year's or her birthday. I mean a good old-fashioned date. A time when the two of you just went out and treated each other to a night that felt like when you first met. Just like a fire needs to re-kindled on occasion to keep it burning, so does your relationship. It is easy to make excuses: the kids have homework, we can't find a sitter, I have a lot of work to prepare for tomorrow. Okay, so plan a date for next week. Work together to make it happen. Keep the fire burning.

Did you tell your wife you love her today?

February 14

"I LOVE YOU"

Did you tell your wife you love her today? Did you tell her yesterday? Is the answer to these questions...Yes? Remember at your wedding when you promised to...Okay, let's lighten up here for a moment. Get in the habit of telling her more than once a day. That way, even on bad days, you may remember to say it at least once. No matter what happens on any given day, tell her you love her. Think of the gifts she has brought to your life. If you have children, your "I love you" is for bringing them into the world. To some, it may sound trite, but the only true response to hearing someone tell you, "I love you," is to respond, "I love you."

Jesus said, "I love you" on the cross. What is your response to that?

Did you tell your wife you love her today?

February 15

A LOVE STORY

You may have never thought of it this way, or maybe no one ever shared it with you, but the Bible is a love story. It is the story of God's love for mankind. First, He created us in His image. Secondly, he made a covenant with us. Then to prove His ultimate love for us, He sent his son to live with us and then die for us. It is simply a story of unending love. It is the greatest story ever told. Yet, it is not complicated. We complicate it.

Say a prayer today for one of the blessings in your life.

February 16
IS MARRIAGE BECOMING OBSOLETE?

For the past fifty years, the number of men and women simply living together has grown exponentially, while the marriage rate has dropped. What can you do about it? Be the best father you can be. It has to start somewhere. Start in your home. Tell your wife you love her. Tell your kids you love them. Do it in front of your children's friends. Some may laugh. Some may act like they didn't hear or see you doing it. Inside, all of them will be influenced by it. Just like when they may see the opposite side of love in their lives, seeing the positive side will leave a mark on them. Maybe, little by little, we will see the marriage rate turn the right direction again. One loving comment at a time.

Did you tell your kids you love them today?

February 17

DO YOU HELP WITH THE COOKING?

Do you like to cook? Do you know how to cook, aside from the things you like to grill? Be sure you share the cooking chores. Heck, today there are so many ready-made items at your grocery store. Pick one of them up, grab a loaf of bread and you are all set. Your kids will be more than willing to help as well. You might even find that the table conversation will be different because your wife will be able to sit and enjoy time with you and the kids. When you give thanks before the meal, you will have given your wife something more to be grateful for. That is a gift in itself.

Did you tell your wife you love her today?

February 18

YOU ARE NOT IN THIS ALONE

Did you get a good night's sleep last night? Did you eat well today? Are you gainfully employed? If you have a positive answer to two or three of these questions, consider yourself blessed. Now, share the wealth! There are countless organizations that perform incredible work for those in our world who are less fortunate. Compassion International, St. Vincent de Paul, Food for the Poor, are a few. There is probably a food bank close to where you live. In short, you have no excuse to not give to those less fortunate than you. You are not in this alone. Share your bounty.

Whose day did you "make" today?

February 19

BE A TEAM MEMBER

All of us have been part of teams throughout our lives. Teams come and teams go, but one team has been in operation since it was formed over two thousand years ago. You have heard of this team. Leading off, we had Andrew and Simon, called Peter. Then James and John. Phillip, Thomas, Bartholomew,... Then, well I suspect you know the members of the original team. What stands out about this team is that they believed in their coach so well that all but one of them died to prove their membership on the team. The last one, we are told, lived to take care of the leader's mother. Membership on this team has ebbed and flowed over the years. Are you on the team?

Did you call or text a message of hope today?

February 20

WEAR THE OTHER GUY'S SHOES

One of the flaws in our human nature is to pass judgement on our fellowman. It is a weakness that leads to all sorts of conflict, much of which can be completely unintended. What leads to our passing judgement on others? Many factors lead to this including: ignorance, greed, jealousy, malice, pride, etc. What measures can you take to curtail passing judgement? It is your responsibility to teach your family how to accept those the Lord has placed in their lives. Take a walk in the other guy's shoes.

Whose day did you "make" today?

February 21

READ

Why is it that so few of us pick up a book and actually read? Especially, in the past thirty years when short bits of information have begun to cloud our everyday lives. Our train of thought is so frequently interrupted that it is hard to concentrate. There is a world of information at your fingertips. Not only will you be enriched, your wife and children may eventually be enriched as well. And...maybe they will follow suit and read a book once in a while. Step out of the so-called information age and discover some thoughts of your own. Read.

Did you tell your wife you love her today?

February 22

GOD'S PLAN FOR EACH SOUL

What have we lost over the centuries due to war, tyrannical behavior or abortion? What have we lost because mankind has killed or abandoned countless millions of souls? What songs have been left unwritten? What cures have never been discovered? How much loneliness have we created by living our own life instead of welcoming new life? How much laughter has been lost? How much love has been lost? Let's let God do the planning and He will leave the living to us.

Say a prayer today for one of the blessings in your life.

February 23
WHO IS RESPONSIBLE FOR TEARING US APART?

Look at the rise of child abuse. Look at legal abortion. Look at the transgressions of ordained clergy, be they Catholic, Muslim, Anglican, etc., thereby taking attention off the 99% of clergy who do God's work. Look at the media playing us against each other, blinding us to what unites us. Who or what is responsible for tearing us apart? It can't be the devil. "He doesn't exist." Believing that is what got us into this mess in the first place.

Say a prayer today for one of the blessings in your life.

February 24

YOU ARE NEVER TOO OLD TO HAVE FUN

One of my more vivid memories as a child was seeing my maternal grandfather putting his hands down my grandmother's back after standing outside watching me shovel six inches of snow off his driveway. He came inside as I drank some hot chocolate that my grandmother had made and startled my grandmother. Surprisingly, she wasn't mad. She was embarrassed that he had done this in front of me, but I will never forget that they laughed like little children. I will never forget their playfulness. This was from people in their early eighties! Don't ever let yourself think you are too old to have fun. I pray that I never do.

Whose day did you "make" today?

February 25

MUSIC BECOMES MEMORIES

There are countless examples of men and women who learned to speak English simply by listening to music. Music creates memories. Think of where your mind goes when you hear a song from your childhood or high school days. Sometimes it seems you can smell the same air you breathed when you heard that song. You children will do the same. Songs sung in the car or heard in the car on your vacation will be memories children will recall years later. Children who learn to read music or play an instrument are typically above average in school. What have you got to lose? Crank it up!

Did you tell your kids you love them today?

February 26

WHAT IS A FAMILY?

Nuclear families, single parent families, extended families and blended families just scratch the surface when we face trying to define a family. What is your definition? Would someone from the outside look at you, your wife and children and say: "That is a family." Being accused of being a family, whatever your family makeup may be, is a badge you can wear with pride. Do your best to wear it well.

Did you tell your wife you love her today?

February 27

THEIR SCHEDULE, NOT YOURS

If you have children, their lives and their schedule supercede yours. You may not like it, but your bowling night, your golf night or your poker night isn't more important than your child's events. Yes, you need a break sometimes, maybe even weekly. But a missed game, recital or school concert won't happen again. Those thirty, sixty or 120 minutes make up a pallet of memories that must include you. Think about it. Do you want to be the dad that everyone notices is never around? Your children will remember. There is golf, bowling or poker to be played another night. Be part of the memories of your children.

Did you tell your kids you love them today?

February 28

HAD A BAD DAY?

Did you have a bad day today? Don't take that bad day home with you. Make it a change of plans night. Pick up some pizza or a bucket of chicken on the way home. Maybe go out and get some ice cream, regardless of the time of year. Make some popcorn and sit and watch a movie with your wife and/or children. Play a game as a family. Do anything to break-up the monotony that some days can bring. Turn your bad day into a shared family night. They don't need to know you had a bad day.

Whose day did you "make" today?

"Nothing vast enters the life of mortals without a curse."

– **SOPHOCLES**

March 1

THE BEST INVENTION EVER

At least from the perspective of the last forty years or so, the cell phone is the best invention ever. You hold in your hand more technology than Neil Armstrong had at his disposal when he went to the moon. Imagine that! You can call anywhere in the world. You can set an alarm. You can keep a calendar. You can call 911 if needed. Find a recipe. Get directions to anywhere you want to go. Call and have food delivered within fifteen minutes. You can order just about anything you need. Oh, and you can talk to a friend, call a long-lost brother or sister on their birthday. All without getting up out of your seat. Where would you be without it?

Did you call or text a friend a message of hope today?

March 2

THE MOST DANGEROUS INVENTION EVER

At least from the perspective of the last forty years or so, the cell phone is the most dangerous invention ever. It can be misused so easily. You can text a message about anybody and say just about anything you want, whether it is true or not. You can get lost in the rabbit hole of the internet. You can engage in hate speech. Most of all, it has robbed us of personal one-on-one conversation. Go to any restaurant and watch couples/families so engrossed in their phones that they don't even talk to each other. It has taken away personal feelings that are shared through meaningful conversation. We may be connected electronically, but not personally. That is a great loss.

Whose day did you "make" today?

March 3

GET OFF THE GRID

How much time do you spend on the internet or starring at your phone or watching TV when you are at home? How much time does your wife spend doing the same thing? Do you allow phones or laptops to be brought to your dinner table? Most of us are oblivious to the time we spend on electronic media. What is that telling our children? You will have no "leg to stand on" trying to unplug your children from their phones or laptops if you are doing the same. Make it a family pact to have limited access to media when that time can be better spent growing as a family. Not just once in a while, but day after day.

Say a prayer today for one of the blessings in your life.

March 4
LONELINESS

In our hyper-connected world, it is sad but true that we are becoming increasingly lonely. The increase in mental health issues of children grows each year. There is no replacement for family and friendship. "Likes" and emojis only provide momentary thoughts of happiness. Hugs and conversations provide necessary human connection. Be aware of your children's and your spouse's level of dependence on artificial technology. Be sure it is not a substitute for human contact. Even if science is able to create an AI robot, it will never replace human contact and human connection. Replace loneliness with human laughter and tears. There is no artificial substitute for either.

Did you tell your kids you love them today?

March 5

DON'T FORCE IT

Today wasn't a good day. Yesterday plainly sucked. Tomorrow doesn't hold much hope either. Feeling like a gerbil on a treadmill? Want to escape from the rat race? We don't always have as much control of our life as we would like. Sometimes it seems that we have no control at all. Then somehow, things turn for the better. Don't force it. Life gets messy sometimes. Things beyond our control interfere. Have courage. Have strength. Have faith. Don't force life. It has an energy of its own. Roll with the challenges of each new day. Take charge when you can. But, don't force it. You are in good hands. His hands.

Say a prayer today for one of the blessings in your life.

March 6

I FEEL INCREDIBLY BLESSED

How did today turn out so well? Yesterday, you thought that there was no way that tomorrow was going to be fun. You had to run here. You had to run there. The dryer stopped working in mid cycle. The rain stopped your outdoor plans. But somehow everything ended up working out. Things seemed to stop before dinner and you actually had time to sit with your wife and have a heartfelt conversation. The sun came out and a gentle breeze was blowing through the windows. Time seemed to stop. How did you get so lucky? Suddenly, you fell so incredibly blessed. Guess what? You are.

Say a prayer today for one of the blessings in your life.

March 7

PHONE USAGE BY CHILDREN

The debate continues as to what age is appropriate to provide a phone for your child. What is more appropriate is setting parameters for the use of the phone. Don't allow a child to use the phone for anything except calling you when they first receive it. Discourage texting. Most of all, limit their access to the phone. They shouldn't be taking a phone to their bedroom with them. And you have the right to see who they have been calling and how often. Track their internet activity. Active children will naturally not always be on their phone, inactive children will abuse the phone privilege. Parental involvement in phone usage is paramount. Without it, your children are left to their own devices. (Pun intended.)

Did you tell your kids you love them today?

March 8

THE RABBIT HOLE

If you have a phone and if you have used it to find information about anything via Google or Facebook or you name the source, it is virtually assured that you have encountered a "rabbit hole." What's a rabbit hole? It's your endless clicking from one story to another and another and another. We see it all around us. People seemingly mesmerized by what they are finding. Rarely will you or anyone remember anything about what they were looking at an hour later. Don't fall in the rabbit hole. Use the time you would have wasted more productively. Have a conversation with a live human being. Go for a walk with your wife. Read a book. Rabbit holes do nothing to enhance your life. Expand your mind or expand your relationship with another human being. There are no rabbit holes in those journeys.

Did you call or text a friend a message of hope today?

March 9

THE SOCIAL DILEMMA
(BORROWING THE TITLE OF A NETFLIX DOCUMENTARY)

Are you struggling with your own or your wife's or your child's addiction to social media? Maybe all of you are suffering together. And there is a chance you don't even realize it. "Social Media is a drug." (- Dr. Emma Lemboh) We have a biological imperative to connect with each other. So, why are we as a society more anxious, more fragile, more depressed? Realizing you are addicted is the first step. Doing something about is the next step. Unplugging may be the only answer if you cannot wean yourselves from the attraction. Watch "The Social Dilemma" on Netflix. It will help you see that you are not alone in this fight.

Whose day did you "make" today?

March 10

UNINTENDED CONSEQUENCES

Continuing our look at social media from yesterday, be sure to keep your eyes open for signs that your children are being overly or overtly influenced due to their exposure to media. It happens to the best of families. Suicide rates are up. Teen driving is dropping. Who would ever have thought that was possible? Kids used to not be able to wait to start driving. Be careful how early you allow your children to have a phone. Monitor closely, very closely, their phone and computer use. Don't allow them to take their computers or phones to their bedrooms. It will be unpopular and your kids will fight you tooth and nail. Be tough as nails and set parameters. Without parameters, you will lose control.

Did you call or text a friend a message of hope today?

March 11

"LIKES" YIKES

How many "likes" did you get today? How many pictures of other people's food did you receive? Okay, so maybe you aren't into keeping track. But do your kids keep track? Chances are they are receiving "likes" or pics from people they have never met and are mistaking them for friendship. Yikes! What is the world coming to? Are we so disconnected that social media dominates our very existence? Start teaching your children when they are young that personal contact cannot be replaced by social media. Love them enough to limit their time spent on computers and cell phones. At first, they make not "like" you for doing so, but over time they and you will notice the difference limited social media exposure had on their lives. Chances are, they will love it!

Did you tell your kids you love them today?

March 12

TICK-TOCK, TIK-TOK

Time is slipping away for too many of us. We are not connecting with each other personally because we are substituting personal time with digital time. Look at those you pass each day. Chances are their personal devices are attracting their attention. Do your children text you instead of calling you? Do you rely on a text or email with co-workers when a personal touch is needed? So many of us no longer even know what a personal touch is. Heaven forbid that we put our words down on paper and share a letter with someone. Time is ticking away. How are you communicating with those around you? Does time pass, Tick-Tock Tick-Tock as you have a personal conversation with someone? Or, are you too busy online, TikTok, TikTok, to notice that anyone is even around?

Whose day did you "make" today?

March 13

KNOW WHO YOUR KIDS ARE HANGING AROUND WITH

The scariest night for any husband and wife is when their kids are going on their first date. Don't suppose, even for a minute that it is totally innocent. Girls as well as boys. The hook-up culture that permeates our society reaches a younger and younger crowd every year. Things you would never have thought to do when you were dating are no longer taboo for a growing portion of society. We can thank the social media explosion for most of it, but ignore it at your own peril. Know who your kids are dating. Introduce yourself to their parents. You don't need to be a detective. Just protective.

Did you tell your kids you love them today?

March 14

SHOW THEM THE WAY

Very little in life is achieved by force. This is especially true when dealing with your children. Showing a child how to do something, sometimes repeatedly, will be more fruitful than forcing them to do it or to learn it by themselves. If you were lucky to enough to have a father in your life, reflect back on the things you learned just by watching. If you like to run, chances are your child will be more apt to try running. If you like to sing, the same holds true. Show a child the way. Lead by example. They may or may not follow. At least you know you tried.

Did you tell your kids you love them today?

March 15

PUT DOWN YOUR PHONE, WRITE A LETTER

We have discussed this earlier this year, but many of you probably didn't follow through. Find a pen and a piece of paper. Write a letter to your wife. Forget about sentence structure or penmanship, just do it. Simply tell her what she means to you. Mention how much you appreciate the mother she is to your children. Add a joke or a favorite line from a movie. Sign it. Place it where she will find it. Done. Now that wasn't so hard, was it?

Did you tell your wife you love her today?

March 16

PROBABLY A PIPEDREAM, BUT WORTH CONSIDERING

Video games and phones should all come with a timer that does not allow you to play them incessantly. They should have a built-in device that after a predetermined amount of time, they simply shut off. Short of that, they should have a quiz, or a video that the user must answer a few questions: history, or math or science related. What harm could come from that? It will be infinitely less harmful than the continued mindless playing of a game or scrolling through a phone. Let's expect more from ourselves and each other

---

Whose day did you "make" today?

March 17

DEVICES AS BABYSITTERS

If you have children, how often do you encourage them to turn on whatever electronic device they have, so that you can go about your day? It may be an innocent attempt to prepare dinner or find time for a leisurely shower or time to clean-up the house. Completing those tasks is important. Just be sure that you don't rely on a touch pad or computer as a regular habit. Creative play should be encouraged over electronic devices.

Did you tell your kids you love them today?

March 18

BE WITH ME TODAY LORD

Do you need a mantra to get your day started? Does each morning seem like the same as yesterday? Here's a suggestion. Start your day by asking: "Be with me today Lord." Acknowledging our creator's presence in your daily life should help you realize that you are not in this alone. You have a wingman at your disposal. Walking with your wingman will make the day easier. There will be days when you will not have to rely on Him in every moment. But knowing He is there when you need Him will make your step livelier. Your mood will change. If you need to, write it on a post-it note and place it on your mirror. He is with you whether you acknowledge it or not. Let Him know you know He is there.

Say a prayer today for one of the blessings in your life.

March 19

YOU WERE MADE FOR GREATNESS

It's not an original thought. You were not made for comfort, you were made for greatness. Striving for comfort is easy. It's a low bar. Striving for greatness as a husband and father should be your goal. Don't just let life come to you. Grab for the high hanging fruit. Tell your wife what she means to you regularly. Don't leave her guessing. Be the dad who shows up at his kid's events. Get involved. It is so much easier to complain about what others do for your children. Be the dad that other kids want their dad to be. That way you know you will be the father your children want as well. Your wife will walk tall because other kid's moms will wish their husbands were more like you. Greatness, not comfort, comes from work and is richly rewarded.

Did you tell your kids you love them today?

March 20

STATS DON'T LIE

"Barring dysfunctional behavior: 'There is no positive statistic to support the lack of a father in the home.'" *(This was a finding of The Morehouse Conference in 2009.)* Additionally, the conference found that involved dads give kids a much better shot at success. So, you can't be a "coming and going" dad. Be an involved dad. Test yourself. Do you know who your child's teachers are? What TV shows do they watch? What is their favorite color? What is their favorite flavor of ice cream? Do you have a passing grade on these questions? If so, break out their favorite ice cream and sit and have a bowl with them. If not, find the answers before it is too late.

Did you tell your kids you love them today?

March 21

WEEKEND BREAKFAST

For most all of us, with children, weekday breakfasts can be challenging. You need to get to work and the kids need to get off to school. There is little time for anything else. It's okay because we all have been there. Weekend breakfast however should be different. It should be a time to relax and unwind. Don't let your TV be the central focus of weekend breakfast. Even a bowl of cereal can be different if you are sitting next to your child and eating with them. Pancakes and waffles are even better. Be creative with the pancakes. Make them in all shapes and sizes. Don't worry, the pancakes will not always look like what you expected them to but it won't matter. The kids will appreciate the attempt.

Did you tell your kids you love them today?

March 22

MEDIA INFLUENCE

Know what you are listening to and watching. There are marketing experts who have only one goal: To influence the way you think and act. If you leave your house each day, you cannot escape it. If you turn on your television or listen to the radio, you cannot escape it. If you turn on your computer, you cannot escape. And most insipidly your phone probably holds the most influence over you. But you can escape it. Not by merely turning these devices off, but by knowing that whatever message you hear, there is another side of the story. Be sure to open yourself to the other side of the story. Do your utmost to be sure your children are aware of this influence as well. Yours is the most important influence in their lives. You refuse this responsibility at your own risk

---

Did you call or text a friend a message of hope today?

March 23

CHILDREN SHOULD NOT HAVE WORRIES

It is not naturally inherent for a child to worry. Have you ever seen children at play? They haven't a care in the world. Worries are different than fears. Children fear the dark, or snakes or spiders or lima beans *(Authors note)*. Where would their worries come from? Try to be sure their worries don't come from you. Kids can sense when you are worried. Limit their exposure to news stories that expound upon death or injuries. We all have enough worries as adults, let's not compound their worries too soon. And, skip the lima beans, kids not only fear them, they won't eat them. :)

Did you tell your kids you love them today?

March 24

LIGHT OR DARKNESS

As you go through life, there will come times when you must make tough decisions. Some will tell you these decisions are either black or white. I would like to offer that they are choices between light and darkness. When taking a stand, consider whether or not your decision will add light to the world or adversely affect the world. By world, I mean your world. How will it affect your wife, your children, your friends? Maybe you will need to turn down a job offer because it would mean that you must uproot your family to another city. Maybe you will have to choose between friends whose lifestyle differs from your own. Be the light for your wife and children. Choose your friends wisely. Live in the glow of your decision.

Say a prayer today for the blessings in your life.

March 25
HAVING A SHORT MEMORY CAN HELP

Life doesn't always go the way you planned. Sometimes it can be even much better. Appreciate the much better. No one is standing in line to give you recognition. They aren't handing out medals today. But guess what, your wife isn't getting recognition either. So, forget the little transgressions each day can bring. Have a short memory of the small stuff that can throw off the trajectory of each day. Recognize the small stuff your wife does for you daily. Give thanks for her. Tell her you love her. Compliment the dinner she cooked even if it tastes the same as the last time she made. The thing is, she made it. Remember that.

Did you tell your wife you love her today?

March 26

WHERE IS YOUR FAITH LIFE?

Your life is a work in progress. The more you learn, the more you want to know. Your relationship with whatever God you worship is the same. The closer you get to Him, the more you want to know. Keep working at it. The closer you get to Him, the more work you will have ahead of you.

Whose day did you "make" today?

March 27

A PRAYER

Dear Lord,
Open my heart to your longing for me.
Help me listen to those you place in my life.
May my response to what I hear be selfless and generous.
May the personal gift of my experience guide me.
And may love be part of my every response.

Did you call or text a friend a message of hope today?

March 28

CALL ME SQUARE

Regardless of your religious belief, the people in our lives who are the most god-like are often looked at as strange. They are in good company. Most great saints were looked at as strange. Some until years after their death. Others, however, became beacons to those around them and formed religious orders, founded hospitals, started schools, and took in the poorest of the poor and cared for them. You may be looked at as square for following your call. Are you willing to shout: "I accept it if you call me square, I am in good company."

Whose day did you "make" today?

March 29

ARE YOU ONE OF THE LUCKY ONES?

When did you first begin to know that you were loved? Sure, you hugged your parents as a child and for the most part followed their direction. But now, don't you find yourself doing a lot of the same things your parents did and think to yourself, "I have become just like my parents'? Count yourself fortunate. Over 90 % of the worst drug users don't have a father in their lives. The number of felons in jail who do not have a father figure in their lives is over 80%. Bobby Bowden, former college football coach, recognized that "roughly 75% of the young men I coached did not have a father in their lives. I shared scripture with them because no man in their lives ever had."

The task of raising children should not fall squarely on the shoulders of mothers. Today, if you still have a father and/or mother in your life, please do two things. First, thank God for them in prayer. Second, call them and tell them you love them. You are among the lucky who can.

Did you tell your kids you love them today?

March 30

IT'S WORTH IT

Has it been a long week? Does it seem like you haven't connected with your wife in quite a while? Does it seem like there isn't time to even carry a conversation for more than ten seconds? But then Saturday night comes. The kids are either asleep or they are otherwise occupied depending on their age. Then, you get the look from your wife. The look that's says: "We got this." You sit beside her and suddenly you look into her eyes like it was the first time you fell in love. The thought hits both of you squarely in the eye: "It's worth it." No matter what each day may bring. No matter how busy the past week was. You know that everything you are doing for each other and your children means something. It's worth it. Don't ever forget that.

Did you tell your wife you love her today?

March 31

MORE THAN THE 'ROUND MOUND OF REBOUND'

I suppose Charles Barkley will forgive me for using a moniker from his basketball days. Mr. Barkley is famous for a Nike commercial he made over twenty-five years ago, in which he stated: "I am not a role model." He took a lot of flack for the commercial but if you really listened and then watched interviews with him after the airing of the commercial, he explained that he was trying to get kids to realize that everyone cannot grow up to be a professional athlete. He encouraged kids to dream about all of the possibilities in their lives, just not professional sports. We could use more Charles Barkleys who speak to kids about being the best they can be at whatever they choose.

Whose day did you "make" today?

"The same God who destined the apostles to be alive at that time destined you and me to be alive at this time."

– FR. JOHN RICARDO

April 1

MAKE PLANS FOR SUMMER

For most families, summer is the season to spend time together. The older your children are the busier your summer will be. So be prepared. Sit down with your wife and plan some activities for the summer. Not all of these activities need to be costly. Plan on some fun activities in and around where you live. Some may require reservations, so keep that in mind as you plan. Let your kids in on the discussions as well. They will enjoy suggesting places to go. It's even okay to be sure some activities are educational. Your kids may complain at first, but even educational activities can turn out to be a highlight of your summer. Don't fail to plan. Or, you may find yourself left out of the fun.

Did you tell your wife you love her today?

April 2

WHO IS YOUR JUDAS?

In spite of your best intentions, there is invariably someone who either has a better idea how to do things or simply wants to tear you down. In the New Testament, when Judas turns against Jesus, it states that the devil entered him. Unfortunately, despite your intentions, there will be those who disagree with you. If you are convinced you are correct, press on. Just know that no matter how true your intentions are, someone may try to tear you down. The truth will win in the end. Be ready for a fight. The devil hates the truth.

Say a prayer today for one of the blessings in your life.

April 3

SIT BACK AND WATCH WHAT YOU CREATED

There will come a time when your children begin to find interests of their own. From a young age, if you teach your children how to be creative and interact with other kids, they will begin to do things on their own. If you are so lucky as to see this happen, just sit back and be proud. It will happen because you and your wife have laid sufficient groundwork for this independent play/thinking to begin. Offer your wife a "high five." Maybe even have a drink to celebrate. Sit back and look at what you have created. Then thank God for allowing you to be part of life's longing for itself.

Did you tell your kids you love them today?

April 4
FAMILIES

Whether you come from a small or large family, you have been shaped by the experience. Sure, a lot of families have prodigal sons or daughters (maybe you are one of the former). But there is not one of us who doesn't owe at least a bit of gratitude to our brother(s) and sister(s). Regardless of your life experience, you are who you are because of how you were formed by your immediate family. For the vast majority of us this formation helped to shape us into the man we are today. When was the last time you spoke to your brother(s) and sister(s)? Have you prayed for them lately? Are you estranged from one or more members of your family? Maybe today is the day to end that estrangement. Take the first step. It will be the hardest. The rest may be a lot easier than you think.

Did you call or text a friend a message of hope today?

April 5

NO SUCH STATISTIC

There is no stat that you can find that supports the lack of a father in the home. Go ahead and look. Along the way, you will find countless statistics that show the negative side of a child not having a father in their life. And yet, the government and social service agencies do little or nothing to support an intact family unit. Fathers must fend for themselves to find attention for what they bring to the family unit. Do everything you can to not be a negative statistic. It will be a positive for not only your children and your wife, it may even help turn the statistics around for those who see what an intact family unit looks like.

Did you tell your kids you love them today?

April 6

THE PROBLEM IS OBVIOUS, THE SOLUTION IS ELUSIVE

You don't have to look far to see that the family unit is held with less esteem than in the past. It has slowly eroded over the past fifty years or so. For a moment, let's concentrate on what can be done to "right the ship." Fathers need to lead the way. Society looks at mothers as being the glue in most families. Fathers, don't be a weak link. Fulfill your duty as a dad. Admittedly, it is seldom easy. But with practice it does become less of a daunting task. You have to work at it to get it right. The examples of fathers who are absent are all around you. You can't be a father just some of the time. Be a 24/7 father.

Did you tell your kids you love them today?

April 7
LARGE FAMILIES

Okay, admit it. You encounter a family that has six, seven, eight or more kids and you think: "not me." It's okay to think that, but don't you have a hint of respect for the parents of a large family? Think about your own sacrifice then multiply that by two, three or four and you begin to understand why large families are such a marvel. Some may even think of large families as some of us think of dinosaurs. But with humans, we must be different. We cannot allow large families to be a memory in history. Celebrate the gift of love that the children of a large family radiate. We can all learn from that. It's a lesson worth learning.

Say a prayer today for one of the blessings in your life.

April 8

THERE IS NO ONE WAY

Do you have more than one child? Do you have two? Three or more? Regardless of how many children you may have, know that as many children as you have, you will need just as many ways to relate to them. Boys are different than girls. Your eldest is different than your youngest. As you are raising them, by developing relationships with your children, you will have a keener sense of what makes each one different. Celebrate those differences. Be sure they know that you have their backs. That way, when you really need each other, getting to the root of the problem may not be so difficult.

Did you tell your kids you love them today?

April 9

FAMILY HISTORY

Children love to hear stories. They love true stories. Your family has a story to tell. And it's true. Tell them about their grandparents and great grandparents. Heck, if you know the history, tell them about your great-great-grandparents. However mundane or hallowed those memories may be, share them with your children. In todays disconnected world, connect your children to real stories. Share pictures with them to bring the stories to life. Then, let their imagination take hold. They will ask questions and before you know it, a bond will be formed that will last until they share it with their children and so on and so on. Eventually, you will be the great grandparent in the pictures that are shared. Imagine the stories they will tell.

Did you tell your kids you love them today?

April 10

BEING A FAMILY CAN BE HARD

Do you have brothers and sisters? Chances are your relationship with some of your siblings are not what you imagined when you were younger. Every family dynamic is different. Unfortunately, despite your best efforts, you may have a brother or sister that you rarely talk to. If there are unsettled differences among you, work to settle them but know that it takes both of you to want to reconcile for it to happen. If it doesn't, suck it up and move on. You did what you could. You have your own life to live whether they wish to be part of it or not.

Say a prayer today for one of the blessings in your life.

April 11

THEY'LL LEARN WHAT THEY SEE

Studies show that pornography can have the same effect as a drug. It can become habitual very quickly. Maybe even after a first glance. It's the greatest source of income on social media. It pervades our society like the worst illness imaginable. Don't think for a second that you can be immune to it. Marriage counselors will tell you that pornography, used by women, as well as men, has ruined countless marriages and as a result, even countless more lives. The depersonalization of our lives leads to viewing porn as an outlet. Don't stick your finger in the outlet. You will get burned.

Did you tell your wife you love her today?

April 12

10,000 TIMES

Have you ever wondered how Michael Jordan got to be so good at basketball? Or how Tiger Woods got so good at golf? Or how St. Mother Teresa became a saint? Practice. Good old-fashioned practice. Trainers and spiritual directors will tell you that repetition is the key to success. Golf coaches will tell you that to work on perfecting your swing you need to practice 10,000 swings. St. Mother Teresa started every day with an hour of adoration. Michael Jordan practiced his shot incessantly, and as he will tell you, he missed more shots that he made. Want to be good at something? Practice.

Did you call or text a friend a message of hope today?

April 13

THE MOMENT YOU FIRST FELT REAL LOVE FOR YOUR CHILD (CHILDREN)

Of course, you loved your child from the moment of his/her birth. But, when did you really feel true love for them? Chances are it was when they were sick for the first time. Or you heard a story of a child who had died and you couldn't imagine it happening to your child. Maybe it didn't hit you until they went to school for the first day or they shared a funny moment that morphed into a moment you know you will share forever. Recognizing these moments make life worth living. It will help make hard times a little easier. Chances are you help make it happen. Recognize and share the love around you.

Did you tell your kids you love them today?

April 14

YOU LOVED THEM BEFORE THEY WERE BORN

If you have children, it's a good bet that you loved them before they were born. The anticipation of their birth filled your entire family. Then when they were born, your life changed in ways you never expected. You now had someone to die for. Sounds a lot like what God felt like before you were born. "Before I formed you in the womb, I knew you" (Jer. 1:5). God sent his Son, to die for you before you were born. Imagine how much love that took.

Did you tell your kids you love them today?

April 15

LOOK 'EM IN THE EYE

Kids can see right through if you are going through the motions. Get down and get dirty with your kids. If they are drawing, grab a crayon. If they are painting be sure to end up with some on your hands. If they want to dance, show them your steps, even if you don't have any. If they want to wrestle or be tickled, get down on the floor with them. Look into their eyes. See the future. See the joy. If you spend time with your kids, they will remember it the rest of their lives. Be a memory, not an afterthought.

Did you tell your kids you love them today?

April 16

YOUR CHILDREN EARN RESPECT

Just as you deserve respect from your children, they deserve respect from you. Treat them like they have personal values that each human acquires through accepted behavior. Acknowledge when they do good and serve others. Admonish them when they stray from accepted behavior. Start young and these accepted behaviors will become second nature. Respect is earned. Yours for them, theirs for you.

Did you tell your kids you love them today?

April 17

RESPECT IS MORE THAN EARNED

The old adage that respect is earned is definitely true. But respect is also taught. It is a father's duty to respect his wife and children. It also applies to how he treats his mother and father. If you are blest to have one or both of your parents in your life, the way you talk and interact with them will be evident to your children. If you treat your parents with respect and love, your children will do the same. Include your children's grandparents in family gatherings. Watch how your children gravitate to them. It is a natural response. That respect will then be reflected in how they treat others in their lives.

Say a prayer today for one of the blessings in your life.

April 18

ENCOURAGE MODESTY

Take a look around at what girls are wearing or not wearing these days. The old saying "You are not going out looking like that," seems to be a thing of the past. We have already talked about respecting your children. Part of that respect is encouraging modesty. Sure, you will get looks of disdain from your daughter(s) but team up with your wife to encourage your kids to not be pulled into wearing what has become culturally acceptable. Set limits.

Did you tell your kids you love them today?

April 19
WHOSE DREAMS ARE THEY CHASING?

Remember when your children were born? All sorts of dreams for them ran through your mind. You were going to keep them safe. You were going to shield them from sorrow. You thought they were going to be artists, or musicians or sports stars. Then, over time, your dreams for them changed. But guess what? They have dreams for themselves as well. Be sure to talk about their dreams. Challenge them to think them through. If they can articulate their dreams and they are different than yours, don't force your dreams on them. Chances are, this will allow both of you to celebrate reaching these dreams as they mature. Dream on, together.

Did you tell your kids you love them today?

April 20
SPRING

Depending on where you live, the start of spring typically is in bloom by late March to early April. Whenever spring starts, be ready for it. Get outside with your children. Get dirty. Pack a picnic lunch. Go for a walk. The new life of spring can bring new life to your family. Time spent outdoors is never wasted. It frees the mind and allows kids to explore. Open their minds and their hearts will follow.

Say a prayer today for one of the blessings in your life.

April 21
CHORES

Harmony in your household is of utmost importance. Your children need to see that mom and dad are on the same page. One way to keep harmony around your house is to treat all chores as "our" chores. Sure, there will be things that you always do and things your wife always does. But, every once in a while, you can surprise your wife and go do the grocery shopping or brush your child's hair. Or, if you avoid painting or doing the wash, pitch in and give it a try. Believe me, your children will notice and so will your wife.

Did you tell your kids you love them today?

April 22
RESPECT YOUR WIFE

You fell in love with her. Probably a type of infatuation at first and then you grew to love her for what she began to mean in your life. As time went on, you grew to love her faults as well. (You have many of your own.) That's a sign of respect. Those around you will watch how you treat your wife. Do you open a car door for her once in a while? Do you let her enter buildings ahead of you? Do you listen to her and not try to complete sentences for her? That's respect. Your children will see how you treat your wife and they will follow suit. If they don't show respect, well, that's a story for another day.

Did you tell your wife you love her today?

April 23

RESPECT YOUR CHILDREN

As your children grow older, you will have to begin treating them differently. You should expect respect if you give respect. Tell them they are doing well when you see them doing something that makes you proud. Be gentle when they stray, but not too gentle. This is a fine line. If you constantly reprimand them, maybe you need to temper your expectations. If they have a favorite activity, be it sports or reading or theatre, take interest in it. But don't be fake about it. If you are somewhat lacking in the knowledge of their chosen activity, tell them so. Most kids will actively show or explain an activity if you show genuine interest. It is a reflection of their love for you and your love for them.

Did you tell your kids you love them today?

April 24

RESPECT THE FEMALE BODY

The most prevalent online activity across the world is pornography. Men and women watch for countless reasons. Is it a lack of knowledge of the harm to not only themselves but to those involved in peddling it? First, make sure you are not attracted to it. Don't downgrade your wife or daughter's sexuality in any way. Doing so lowers their self-esteem and your other children as well. Second, don't hang around guys who talk about it or want to share it with you. Be firm in your disdain for all aspects of degrading the female body. Imagine your daughter being involved in pornography. You wouldn't want it for her. Don't support it for anyone else.

Whose day did you "make" today?

April 25
FROM THE STREETS OF CALCUTTA

Little was known of Agnes Gonxha Bojaxhiu until her 38th year. She heard "a call within a call" and founded a home for the destitute and dying in India. She slept on a wood floor for most of her adult life. She spent at least an hour in prayer to start each day. Her simplicity of heart and love of Our Lord's suffering children has inspired millions. Because of her efforts she won a Nobel Prize for Peace. As she ended her acceptance speech she said: "And let us all join in that one prayer, God give us courage to protect the unborn child, for the child is the greatest gift of God to a family, to a nation and the whole world. God bless you." St. Mother Teresa rose from Calcutta and changed the world. Shine to your family first. Who knows, maybe a nation will follow.

Did you call or text a friend a message of hope today?

April 26

...DOESN'T MEAN YOU SHOULD

Words matter. And yes, there is free speech in this great land of ours. But just because you can say something doesn't mean you should. This is most evident in entertainment circles, especially among comedians, but it filters into society at large. However, you use words at your own peril. There may be no more difficult occupation than being an expletive free, no sex-referencing stand-up comedian. Few have mastered the technique because it is so easy to make a decent living by saying whatever you please. I contend the best jokes are those that make you think. Although, that is something those defined as part of the lowest common denominator may not understand. For that is what it has become. Success is determined by catering to the lowest common denominator. Let's strive to set the bar higher.

Whose day did you "make" today?

April 27
CHEF DADDY

Who does the cooking around your house? If you are the primary "chef," good for you. If you are not, maybe it's time you learned. Don't be fooled by all of the competition cooking shows on TV. Cooking is relatively simple if you start with the basics. You will be surprised how little time it takes to put a nutritious meal on the table for your family. Remember, practice makes perfect and start simple. Most kid's love spaghetti or noodles, so find recipes that have spaghetti or noodles in them. A simple tomato sauce with some diced tomatoes mixed in is an instant hit. Pick-up a loaf of bread on your way home to compliment the sauce and you are on your way.

Did you tell your kids you love them today?

April 28

YOUR WORLD CAN BE A LONELY PLACE

It has been said that the world can be a lonely place. Is that a description of your world? Have you felt that maybe your world can at times seem like a lonely place? Maybe it's because you want your world to be your way. Need a hint to make it less lonely? Make it a place that you do things together. Your life will suddenly seem less dark. Human beings need contact with other human beings. Doing things together with your wife, children or friends will brighten your world. The choice is yours.

Did you call or text a friend today a message of hope?

April 29

ITS HARD TO BE A FATHER

You signed up for the job. That doesn't mean you are qualified for it. Nobody checked your credentials. But you are a dad every day. Days when you would rather stop by the bar for a drink with the guys. Days when all you want to do is crash on the couch and watch a ballgame. Days when you could care less if the lawn is overgrown. But your son has a runny nose. Your daughter needs help with her homework. And your wife is helping her sister who needs a shoulder to cry on. Suck it up. Tomorrow will come with troubles of its own. Shoulder the challenges of today. Believe it or not, you will be better for it.

Did you tell your kids you love them today?

April 30

GAMALIEL WAS RIGHT

When you take sides in a fight, know what it is that you are fighting against. The disciples of Jesus refused to be silenced by the rulers of Jerusalem. Gamaliel, one of the Pharisees, warned his brethren not to try to silence the truth, warning that in doing so, it may spread even wider. His advice was not heeded. When you face opposition, be sure you know who the enemy is and what they are fighting for. If you don't recognize your enemy, you may not understand that he has more weapons and strength than you. Your fight may become futile. Know what you are fighting against. Some battles are better left unfought.

Say a prayer today for one of the blessings in your life.

"Education is not merely neglected in many of our schools today, but is replaced to a great extent by ideological indoctrination."

– **THOMAS SOWELL**

May 1

EXPECT MORE FROM THOSE WHO TEACH YOUR CHILDREN

It is your responsibility as a parent to know what your children are being taught in school. If you are made aware of things that you do not agree with, speak up. Silence can be deadly. Let your children's teachers know you are listening. If you are certain that what your children are being taught goes against your moral judgement, speak up. Band together with other parents who feel the same way. You only get one chance to raise your children. Being silent is abdicating the raising of your children to those with whom you disagree. Expect more from the educators of your children. Don't be silent. SPEAK UP!

Did you tell your kids you love them today?

May 2

LOVE YOUR CHILDREN WITH THE TRUTH

You only have a short number of years to raise your children. You don't have time to waste on making up for lost time, or for making up for mistakes in judgement, or for living the truth. Commit to loving your children by always telling the truth. They will learn it by osmosis. Unfortunately, they will also learn the opposite if taught or shown it. Love your children with the truth. Besides your love, it is the greatest gift you can give them.

Did you tell your kids you love them today?

May 3

THEY LEARN WHAT THEY SEE

Do you think your kids aren't watching you? Do you think they aren't listening to you? They not only watch you, they want to be just like you. A young boy or girl will run along with mom or dad every chance they get. They will sing the songs you sing. They will use the words you use. Do you want them to match your every step? What do you watch on TV? What do you read? How do you spend your spare time? Without you even noticing, they will want to do the same. Lead by example, not with words. Your kids will learn what they see.

Did you tell your kids you love them today?

May 4

TELL YOUR KIDS 10,000 TIMES

There are 365 days in a year. If you tell your children you love them once a day for 27+ years, you will reach 10,000. Twice a day takes less than 14 years. Sounds like a goal that is reachable. No one is going to keep track of the count, but the times you forget may be remembered. Including a hug never hurts either. If you forgot today, set this book aside and tell them right now. You don't have to read the next page until tomorrow.

Did you tell your kids you love them today?

May 5

LEARN TO SAY NO

We have forgotten how to say "no." This is especially true of parents. They want to treat their children as friends. Soon, their children aren't shown authority. Authority matters. Respect matters. True authority matters. Government and media voices have muddled authority. We want our own way. We are conditioned not to accept "no" as an answer. You probably don't have to look too far around you to see signs of this. Single parents and divorced parents can more easily fall into the trap that leads to a softening of authority. Teach your children the meaning of "no" from an early age. You may think they won't love you if you say "no." Love them by saying "no."

Did you tell your kids you love them today?

May 6

MOTHER'S DAY COMING UP

Mother's Day is fast approaching. What are your plans? If your mother is still alive, be sure to at minimum give her a call. A visit is even better. Presents are nice, but your presence is what she will most appreciate. If your children are young, help them show their mother how much they love her. They may need your help. Keep it simple. Your wife will 'gush' over whatever they do. And don't use the excuse that she is not your mother so that you do not have to do anything for her on Mother's Day. She is the mother of your children. That is all the reason you need to show how much you appreciate the gift she is to not only your children's lives, but your own.

Did you tell your wife you love her today?

May 7

RECOGNIZE THE NEEDS OF YOUR SPOUSE

We are all too busy. Our lives can be overly stressful. Sometimes you need a break. Be honest with your wife and ask her to be honest with you. If the last thing you need tonight is more stress, tell your spouse you need a break. It will be better for your entire family when the two of you recognize the needs of each other. The kids don't have to know. Work it out between the two of you. Recognizing each other's needs will be a gift to each of you and your children.

(Remedies for relieving the stress mentioned above can be as simple as watching your favorite comedy or going for a lonnnggg walk. Maybe your wife just needs a soaking bath and a glass of wine. Find your own remedies for the sake of you and your family.)

Did you tell your wife you love her today?

May 8

TELL YOUR WIFE 10,000 TIMES

How much do you love your wife? Do you work at it every day? Did you tell her you love her this morning? Did you tell her when you went to bed last night? Do you ever call or text her during the day to share a message, just for the heck of it. Don't keep track, but just like any human activity, it takes practice. Love is the most fleeting emotion on earth. It takes constant practice to perfect. Strive for perfection.

Did you tell your wife you love her today?

May 9

ALONE TIME FOR MOM

From time to time, husbands should help their wives have some alone time for themselves. It can be as simple as giving her time to have a relaxing bath or shower. Time to paint her nails. Maybe she needs a day of shopping or a few hours to take a long walk. If she has friends she hasn't connected with for too long, encourage her to schedule time to meet up with them. Sometimes an overnight or weekend getaway with friends may be in order. Communicate with your wife to be sure she gets time to unwind. There is nothing wrong with this. In fact, it will be healthy for both of you.

Did you tell your wife you love her today?

May 10

MAKE YOUR OWN SPECIAL DAY

Hallmark and FTD will be upset with you, but aside from her birthday and Mother's Day, you don't have to be influenced by recognizing made-up holidays throughout the year. You do however have 363 days each year to tell your wife how much she means to you. Again, keep it simple. Just by you doing something out of the ordinary, she will love whatever you do. If she likes to sleep in on weekend mornings, let her do that. Maybe she would like you to make breakfast or dinner. Or go for a walk. If she likes time alone to read, make sure she has the opportunity. Watch her favorite movie with her. Maybe you could tell her your love her more than once a day. The choices are endless and the rewards will last and last.

Did you tell your wife you love her today?

May 11

LOVE HER ANYWAY

Okay, so lately things have not been a bowl of cherries. Life has thrown you a curve or two. You may find yourself coming and going. It is easy to take the relationship with your wife for granted. Don't let busy times distract you from what matters most. Be sure to love your wife through thick and thin. You are going to look back on this time as a blip that will fade away. No matter what each day brings, when it comes to your wife, love her anyway. Repeat after me ... LOVE HER ANYWAY!

Did you tell your wife you love her today?

May 12

THEY ARE LISTENING

How did you greet your wife this morning? How did you greet her when you came home this evening? Did you tell her you love her? Did your kids hear you tell her? Just as your kid's are always watching you, they are listening as well. Don't think for a second that just because they may be in another room that they don't hear. Make sure you tell your wife you love her. Be sure to tell your children as well. On bad days the language you use can erase any good memories they had of yesterday's language. Make sure any disagreements you have with your wife are handled fairly and in a tone that will not alarm your children. It is human nature to disagree once in a while. Just be civil about it. They are listening.

Did you tell your kids you love them today?

May 13

ROLE MODELS

The older you get, the more you realize that the best role models are either in the same house as yours or maybe a neighbor or someone you worship with at your church. Rarely are role models on the silver screen or on your TV or on social media. Countless 'so called' celebrities or sports figures have been held up as role models until we hear about their foibles or falls from grace. Guess what, they are human too. They are looking for role models just like you. Believe it or not, you are role models to them. They strive for direction just like the rest of us. Look to those around you for direction. You probably don't have to look very far.

Say a prayer today for one of the blessings in your life?

May 14

BE A ROLE MODEL

If you have children, guess what, you are a role model. It comes with the territory. In your children's formative years, you have the most direct influence on them. Don't allow their teachers or coaches to unduly influence them. Be the man your son's and daughter's friends look up to as well. Sure, it is a lot of responsibility, but shirking this responsibility and allowing your children to look elsewhere for direction can be a recipe for disaster. By being a role model, you will garner respect from those around you. It is only by hard work that any respect is earned in life.

Did you tell your kids you love them today?

May 15

RAISE SELFLESS CHILDREN

What is the best way to raise selfless children? Let them see you be selfless. Your actions will speak louder to them than you might ever imagine. "You don't have to do great things. Just small things with love." (To paraphrase St. Mother Theresa) Don't honk your horn or yell at others on the road. Open doors for others when entering a store. Donate to charities. Let your kids see that you are doing it. Encourage them to volunteer at school when asked. Volunteer at a soup kitchen. And make it a year-round thing. The needy are not just needy around the holiday season.

Whose day did you "make" today?

May 16
THEY ARE WATCHING

Do you know what kids are better at than you may give them credit for? They are watching you. Have you had a bad day? Can your kid's sense that as soon as you walk in the door? Do your actions toward your wife and family send off the wrong signals? Simply put, if you are stressed, your wife and kids will sense it. We all have to deal with it from time to time. Just be sure it doesn't become standard operating procedure. Continued stress is not good for you physically and mentally. The same is true of its effect on you family. Be conscious of how you act. They are watching and will mimic you if you aren't careful.

Did you tell your kids you love them today?

May 17

A CARDINAL RULE

Never, never, ridicule someone in a public setting. NEVER. The worst way to hurt anyone is to do it in front of others. Especially your children. No matter how hurt or disappointed you may be with your child, save the speech for later. We see it all too often in society. Not only will it look bad for your child, it will look worse for you. You can lose instant respect by bringing someone down in front of others. Typically, your reaction is based on your own bad day or situation. Don't take it out on your kid. The result could be held against you for years. An instant of ridicule can last forever. So can an instant of caution. Choose the latter.

Did you tell your kids you love them today?

May 18

ONE-ON-ONE TIME

Parents, both moms and dads, should spend one-on-one time with each of their children. This is not favoritism. It is an opportunity to enjoy simple time together. Depending on your child's interests, try to find something that matches their interest. It will allow you to see a side of your child that you may not see if done with the entire family. You will probably hear different things in your conversations as well if it is just the two of you. Spouses should work together to schedule this one-on-one time periodically. It is essential to the growth of a healthy family. (If you are a parent that travels a lot, this time can help you catch up with what your children are involved in.)

Did you tell your kids you love them today?

May 19

TEAMING UP TO PLAY VIDEO GAMES

Do your pre-teen and teenage children play video games "on-line." Do you know who they are playing the games with? If you don't know, you should. There have been countless stories of "on-line" video game "friends" becoming much more than just friends. Just as when your children start dating, get to know who your children are hanging out with, 'on-line' and off. They may not understand and they may protest, but it is your responsibility as a parent to watch who and what your child (children) are exposed to.

Did you tell your kids you love them today?

May 20

VIRGINITY IS NOT A DISEASE

Since the "Free Love" mindset came into vogue in the late sixties, the idea of losing your virginity, for both males and females, has become acceptable behavior. It's not. Just as dressing modestly should be encouraged, fathers need to talk with their sons and mothers need to talk with their daughters, from a young age, to teach them what a gift their body is and not to give into the social pressure. Maybe even teaching that virginity is not rare would be start. The human body is a temple. It should be treated as such. Start when they are young so that they know what a gift their body is. It is not to be given away except in matrimony. It will probably be the toughest task that you as a parent will face. Face it head on.

Did you tell your kids you love them today?

May 21
PROSTITUTION

Some joke that it might be the oldest profession. It's no joke. The damage done to the mental health of women involved in prostitution is only magnified by the prevalence of it across society. The jock culture is riddled with it. It's a "guy" thing they like to say. No, it's a "girl" thing. It's has ended countless marriages and relationships. It tears apart hearts and souls. It leaves women lonely and scarred. Don't joke about it even a little. Imagine your daughter being involved. Unimaginable right? Then it is just as unimaginable for any other guy's daughter being involved in it as well.

Did you tell your kids you love them today?

May 22

OPEN YOUR HOME TO YOUR CHILDREN'S FRIENDS

Want to add a layer of protection for your children? Get to know their friends, so they get to know you. Have summertime get togethers in the backyard. If you have a basement, let them have some fun messing around. But you have every right to check up on their activity. Again, don't be a detective. Have fun with your kids and their friends. They will get to know you and you will get to know them. Be firm if somehow their activity goes beyond your boundaries. They will respect you for being firm. Chances are, if you play your cards right, you may develop relationships with some of these kids for life.

Did you tell your wife you love her today?

May 23

THE BEST THINGS IN LIFE ARE FREE

Think about the moments in your life that you felt the most joy. When you thought, "life can't get better than this." Chances are those moments included your wife and/or children, or close friends. They most likely occurred when you were holding someone or laughing with someone or enjoying the company of family and friends. Your wedding night, the birth of your children, watching your son or daughter score their first goal or make their first basket all provide moments that you will recall for years to come. Simple moments in life that are best savored together. These are the best things in life. Help make them happen. When they happen, don't tell me you don't feel free.

Say a prayer today for one of the blessings in your life.

May 24

FIND SOMEONE WHO LOVES YOU

I had an old friend who once remarked in a discussion about finding someone to love who said: "I just want to find someone who loves me." We can spend so much time being someone we are not, trying to find someone to love, when the best way to find someone may be to just be ourselves. This is great advice to share with your children when they are old enough to understand. Finding someone who loves you for who you are will yield better results. Who knew "being" you could be the answer to your search for love.

Did you tell your wife you love her today?

May 25

I'M PROUD OF YOU

How often do you say it: "I'm proud of you?" You know it in your heart, but life passes and we fail to build each other up. Maybe it's because you didn't hear it enough when you were young. New habits are sometimes hard to sustain. Make it your goal to make saying: "I'm proud of you," a habit. Everyone you shower with these four words will be better off for hearing them. The effect of hearing these words may not be apparent each time you say them, but He will know you said them. So that when your days are done and you see Him in His glory, he will say those four words to you. It's something He has a habit of doing.

Did you tell your kids you love them today?

May 26

KIDS CAN HELP AROUND THE HOUSE

They won't want to do it all the time, but teach your kids responsibility around the house. Start by teaching them to put their toys away. When they are old enough, have them put their dishes in the sink. Let them fold wash or separate socks once in a while. Make a game out of it. They will look at it as fun instead of work. Most kids will help around the yard, for a brief time. Teach them to keep track of their shoes. Responsible kids become responsible adults. Something every society needs.

Did you tell your kids you love them today?

May 27

ALONE TIME FOR DAD

Fathers, it is okay to ask for some time for yourself to getaway. It may just be an afternoon. Maybe a day of golf with friends. You could attend a car show or go bowling with some buddies. The point is to unwind so that you will be better for your wife and family when you return. Just as your wife needs time away once in a while, so do you. Only the two of you know each other's needs. Be sure to allow yourselves time to regroup every so often. You, your spouse and your family will be better for it.

Whose day did you "make" today?

May 28

STAY INFORMED

You don't have to participate in the 24/7 news cycle to stay informed. In fact, watching too much of the news cycle can actually be detrimental to 'open' thought. But stay informed. Listen to what your kids are talking about. What dominates the conversation at work? What is your wife talking about that either motivates her or possibly scares her? Stay informed. Life can pass you by if you tune-out. Stay tuned to those around you. You will learn a lot about yourself and them.

Say a prayer today for one of the blessings in your life.

May 29

MAKE BOOKS YOUR OWN

Take time to find good books. Buy a highlight marker and highlight parts that hold your interest. "Dog-ear" pages you might want to refer to in the future. You may even find yourself quoting what you have read. If you find a particular genre that interests you, you may become a quasi-expert. Who would have thought that was possible?

Whose day did you "make" today?

May 30

DON'T WAIT TO DO SOMETHING

"Git 'r done." To coin a phrase. So many of us walk around full of ideas. Hopes and dreams fill our minds. Yet, we seldom act on them, afraid they will be too hard or someone might laugh at us. You only have one chance at this life. Stop putting off what is in your heart. How many men and women went to their graves holding on to unfulfilled hopes and dreams? Don't wait to do something. You may find out that others saw the possibility in you that you did not see. Show the world what you have to offer. Don't wait to do something.

Did you call or text someone a message of hope today?

May 31

WHEN YOU SING, YOU PRAY TWICE

Wherever you worship, sing like no one is listening. Do you ever wonder why people are drawn to sing in choirs? There is a special feeling that can only be experienced if you are part of the choir. It takes practice to make a choir sound just right. You have probably heard choirs that need more practice. Regardless, the choir members offer their song to Our Lord. He hears their efforts and they are blessed accordingly. It is said that there is a choir of angels that has surrounded God from the beginning of time. All they have ever done is sing in His presence. Imagine that feeling. Sing, maybe you will experience it.

Say a prayer today for one of the blessings in your life.

"God comes to you, disguised as your life."

– Paula D'Arcy

June 1

GOD COMES TO YOU DISGUISED AS YOUR LIFE

(PAULA D'ARCY)

"God comes to you disguised as your life." If you aren't sure about these words, think about when you last felt alone. Think about when you weren't sure about a bad decision you made, but then someone or something happened in your life that turned things around. It probably wasn't because of something you did, but it was because who you were around. You don't always create your own destiny. You need a little help. Chances are, if you reflect on it, God had a hand in it. You may hear someone say that something that happened to them was unexplainable. Maybe the unexplainable can be explained as your life with an added presence. It won't seem so disguised the next time.

Say a prayer today for one of the blessings in your life.

June 2

LIVING IN YOUR OWN SKIN

What is it that you would like to change most about yourself? Have you ever felt uneasy living in your own skin? Don't beat yourself up over this because it may become a positive thing that will make you an even better husband, father or friend. Start by asking Our Lord to help you make an assessment of who you are and see what comes to mind. Maybe you could even ask your wife if there is something you can change that will be positive for your relationship. Don't be afraid of the answer, she loves you already anyway.

Did you tell your wife you love her today?

June 3
BRINGING YOUR CHILDREN UP

Your children are the greatest gift you will ever receive. Treat them as such. Tell them you love them. Tell them you are proud of them. And don't just do it in private. If other people: parents, friends, teammates, see you praising them, they may become jealous and even admire you.. It is so rare to hear praise these days. Be rare. Surprise yourself and your kids with praise. Then watch it spread. They may not praise you but they will treat friends that way. And eventually they will treat their spouse that way. And the next generation will be blessed with praise also. All because you treated them as you would want to be treated.

Did you tell your kids you love them today?

June 4
FEELING LONELY?

Our world is longing for human connection. If you are feeling lonely, maybe it's because you want too much of 'your' way. Your ideas aren't seeing the light of day because you are not sharing them. The best way to make life less lonely is to share it with others. When things are less your way and more 'our' way, you will begin to do things together. Your ideas will see the light of day. Then, watch them blossom.

Did you call or text a friend a message of hope today?

June 5
FAMILY FOUNDATION

Whether you are Christian, Jewish, Muslim, Catholic or just about any formal religion, the family has always been held as a foundation of faith. Catholics refer to the family as The Domestic Church. Respect for mothers and fathers permeates the family unit of all religions. So, why is the foundation of the family crumbling? We are letting it be influenced by too many outside voices that see the family as a threat. Just look at the state of the family depicted on TV. It is rare to see a mother and father living together. It is so much easier to make fun of a home. Be proud members of the Domestic Church. That is your responsibility. Don't take that responsibility lightly.

Did you tell your kids you love them today?

June 6
REACH OUT TO A FRIEND

Chances are you have two or three good friends. Chances are you haven't sat down and talked with one or two of them in months. You probably texted them or emailed them, but when was the last time you sat and talked with them? Admittedly, both your life and theirs is busy with work and family. Reach out. Invite them to breakfast, or lunch or a drink after work. Take a chance that maybe they were feeling the same way you are and wanted to reach out to you. Do it today. It's already been too long.

Did you all or text a friend a message of hope today?

June 7

YOUR WIFE NEEDS A DAY OFF

Think about how much you like a day off from work. Now, give your wife a chance to feel the same way. This will take some co-ordination, but look at the calendar and schedule a day off for your wife. Obviously, this will probably be a weekend day, but give it a try. You may need help from a family member or a friend to pull this off, but it will be worth it. By doing so, you will be showing her how much she means to you and how much you are aware of what she has to do on a daily basis. Don't be coy and schedule a day for two years from today. Make it happen, soon.

Did you tell your wife you love her today?

June 8

TIME-OUT

The practice of time-out as a form of discipline for children has been around for years. Because it works. Whether you choose to use the time-out method or another method of discipline be consistent in its enforcement. Friends don't enforce time-out on each other. Parents who love their children do. Don't be your child's friend. As they learn from the correction of a time-out, you will see a change in behavior. Be stern but not overbearing. Don't over use any one method of discipline. Use them at your discretion.

Did you tell your kids you love them today?

June 9

TIME-OUT FOR YOU

Just as a time-out can work on disciplining your children, it can work for you as well. Self-imposed discipline for rash behavior may be necessary at times to calm you or act as a wake-up call. Help each other out as spouses when your behavior is beyond the norm. Suggest a short break from family interaction until you are able to calm yourself. You, your spouse and your children will be better for it.

Did you tell your kids you love them today?

June 10

IT'S GOOD TO BE A DAD

You were able to come home with a smile on your face. The meeting at work went better than you planned. Somehow traffic was lighter than normal. Your wife stopped and bought your favorite ice cream for dessert. Your daughter shows you a picture she drew in school and it actually looks like something. And, on top of that, your son is waiting to shoot some hoops with you. Best of all, it's not a dream. Yesterday's stress is a forgotten memory. This is indeed something to get used to. But buckle up, tomorrow is another day. But at least for today, it feels good to be a dad.

Did you tell your wife you love her today?

June 11
GET OUTDOORS

Pretty much no matter where you live you can find a space for outdoor activity. You and your children need a breath of fresh air on a regular basis. Don't deprive them and yourself the gift of outdoor activity. If you can find a trail with a creek and the weather cooperates, your children can be kept busy for hours. Make a game of it. Challenge them to find different colored or different shaped rocks. Have a rock skipping contest. See how many different kinds of leaves they can find. If it is a moonlight walk, have them point out the brightest stars. Let your imagination take over and watch theirs follow

---

Whose day did you "make" today?

June 12

WARTS AND ALL

Yours is not a perfect family. Everyone will see you, "warts and all." That is not something to be ashamed of. There is no "perfect" family. Every family struggles. Every family manages trials in a singular fashion. It is how you deal with trials that will define you. Don't try to do it alone. Reach out to friends and family when they are struggling so that when you face life's slings and arrows, you will find someone to help you through it. Accept the warts and all of those in your life and they will respond in kind.

Say a prayer today for one of the blessings in your life.

June 13
SADDEST STATISTIC I HAVE EVER HEARD

You may have never thought about it, but it is easier for a child to mourn the loss of a father through death than to have a father who is alive and doesn't want to be a part of their life. If you think about it, it makes perfect sense. Through mourning you can make sense of the loss. But if you know your father and he wants no part of you, that's hard to live with. That is a sense of loneliness that cannot be healed. Where is your child supposed to find that lost sense of someone who cares? (This phenomenon wasn't prevalent until recent years. There have always been fathers who abandoned their children. But the rate is growing larger every day.) Be a dad who is around. However hard it may be. Stop the cycle of loneliness. Your children deserve better.

Did you tell your kids you love them today?

June 14

LET KIDS BE KIDS

Do you ever stop to watch a child at play? Have you watched them concentrate on the smallest detail? Don't you wish you had time to do the same. Let kids be kids. Uninhibited fun is sometimes shared just by watching. You were young once. Remember repeating over and over your favorite game, or re-reading your favorite book? Encourage them to experience new things, but let them decide what catches their interest. You can't force fun, you can only revel in the joy that it brings.

Did you tell your kids you love them today?

June 15

EXPOSE YOUR CHILDREN TO "THE FINER THINGS"

It is intrinsic to the human mind to appreciate beauty. Beauty in people. Beauty in music. Beauty in art. Don't think for a minute that children cannot appreciate beauty as well. Although at certain times, opportunities to share fine art may be difficult to find, it doesn't always cost a lot. Some museums are free or have children's discounts. There is plenty of beauty available to you on whatever streaming service or cable provider you have. If you look for it, you will find it. You will end up enjoying it as well. It's a gift that years from now will reap benefits.

Did you tell your kids you love them today?

June 16

A BIG WIN FOR DAD

Have you been on a date with your wife lately? If not, here is a foolproof way to score points with your wife...BIG TIME! Preferably a Friday or Saturday night. Set a date and time to go out. Find a sitter. It's not that hard! Then tell your wife that she will have time to take a nap, time to take a soaking bath, time to get ready. Three hours is a reasonable time for all of that. Plan to take the kids to a park or a movie. Take them to Mc-Donalds or a pizzeria. This doesn't have to get overly expensive, but how many times are you actually going to be able to do it? You can be guaranteed that your wife will appreciate this more you can imagine. Do it for her...she deserves it. Guess what, you do too.

Did you tell your wife you love her today?

June 17

A DIFFERENT KIND OF FATHERS DAY

Is your father still among us? Has he been part of your life? If he has you are better off than over 50% of the population. The sad truth is that less than half of us lived with our father when we were growing up. What a sad statement on our society. How we got here is a book of its own. But if you lived with your father when you were growing up, call him today and tell him you love him. The man you have become or are becoming is a direct result of your father's influence on your life. Granted, for some of you that may not have been a positive thing to deal with. Either way, you learned how to treat children. Now it is your turn. Be a dad that your kids will want to call years from now on Father's Day and have them tell you that they love you. Maybe we can buck the trend and the majority of future children will have a dad to call on the third Sunday in June.

Say a prayer today for one of the blessings in your life.

June 18

FATHER'S DAY

Yes, it's great to be treated special the third Sunday of June. Especially if you actually put in the time to earn the treatment. But, in reality, don't you feel guilty for being recognized for doing what brings you the greatest joy of your life? Enjoy today. Continue your journey to earn the special treatment again next year.

Whose day did you "make" today?

June 19

A GIFT FOR DAD

There is a true story of a college football linebacker who wasn't a first team member. He wasn't the biggest or the fastest or the strongest. He just showed up everyday and gave it everything he had. Then one day, he showed up and insisted to his coach that he needed to start. The coach listened but denied the request. The linebacker insisted to his coach that today was going to be different, regardless of the opponent. After a few hours of wrangling with the player, the coach relented. The young man told his coach that he would not regret it. He started the game and made the first tackle. He blitzed on the third play and had a sack. On the second series, he had two more tackles and broke up a pass. This continued throughout the entire game. His fellow players didn't even recognize their teammate. He was by far the best player on the field that day. More than perplexed, the coach sat with the linebacker after the game and asked him where this sudden burst had come from. The young man, with tears in his eyes, related that his father had been born blind. He raised four children and worked tirelessly to support his family the best he could. He then said, "My father died two days ago. I realized that today's game would be the first time he ever saw me play. I wanted him to see me at my best."

Did you tell your kids you love them today?

June 20

THE DAD "HALL OF FAME"

Are you in your children's DAD HALL OF FAME? You would hope the answer would be yes for all of us. Considering that there are only a handful votes you need to be enshrined. Will you put in the work? Will you show up when needed? Would you stay eligible for enshrinement? There isn't a jacket to be worn or a trophy to be won. Just the love and admiration of your children. Sounds like enough of a reward to me.

Did you tell your kids you love them today?

June 21

YOU DON'T NEED LUXURIES

Luxuries are ok, in and of themselves, but don't expect simple pleasures out of them. How many people do you know that have rooms of furniture that no one sits in? Or, homes so large that they either cannot fill all of them or once they are filled are never used. It can be too easy to have so many luxuries that they inhibit having fun. Treat yourself to luxuries that you and your family can use. But not so many that you have to spend time maintaining luxuries. Maintain the relationships with your wife and family. That is your greatest luxury. Embrace it.

Say a prayer today for one of the blessings in your life.

June 22

WANT TO HAVE A CATCH?

What is your connection with each of your children? Many of us are familiar with the line from the movie, *Field of Dreams*, "Dad, do you want to have a catch?" Maybe your daughter likes to sing or play volleyball. Maybe your son likes to run or read a book. Know what it is that they like to do and take interest in it. You don't have to be good at it, but make the connection. They want the connection just as much as you do. Don't force it, but don't let time pass and you grow apart. Keep the connection alive. It will make each of your lives better.

Did you tell your kids you love them today?

June 23

THE TRUTH DOES SET YOU FREE

Have you ever been caught in a lie? Depending on the size of that lie, it may have taken you some time to recover from it. Did you learn your lesson? Unfortunately, some people never learn. They think that they can take the easy road to success and/or happiness. Only to find out that they are deeper into a lie as time goes by. The lie is like a stone around their neck. Tell the truth. It can set you free. It will help you soar in the eyes of your fellow man. Happy flying!

Whose day did you "make" today?

June 24

SEAT OF YOUR PANTS APPROACH

Where do you find out how to be a father? You may be one of the lucky ones who had a father that loved you and can fall back on what you remember about how he raised you. Or, you had a strong mother who did the same. If you are lucky enough to have had both, you should have a pretty good base to work from. If not, look around for role models who will help you. However, in spite of whatever you were taught or picked up by observations over the years, there are going to be times in your life when you will have to use the "seat of your pants" method. What's that you ask? It will be spur of the moment or downright serious challenges to your daily walk on this earth. Whenever you find yourself having to make such decisions, sometimes all you can do is pray. Come to think of it, that may be the best place to start.

Did you call or text a friend a message of hope today?

June 25

YOU'RE GOING TO SCREW UP

Face it, you are not always going to be at your best. You are going to screw up. Be sure it is just the little things that you screw up. And when you do, admit it and move on. Don't make a bad situation worse. Too many times our ego gets in the way and we take a stand when that is the worst thing you can do. The truth hurts sometimes. You are not perfect. The sooner you realize this, the happier you are going to be. It's okay to screw up. Be a man, admit it and move on.

Say a prayer today for one of the blessings in your life.

June 26

VIDEO GAMES...SET PARAMETERS

If you are like most parents these days, without even realizing it, you either have or are in the process of using an electronic device: iPad, video pad, touch pad of some sort, to garner the attention of your child/children so that you can have a few moments of peace. Watch out! You may be encouraging future activity that can turn into addiction to video games. Be sure you know what your children are doing when you are not watching. It's important to monitor what kind of games they are playing. And most importantly, limit the amount of time they are playing.

Did you tell your kids you love them today?

June 27

IF YOU DON'T KNOW HOW...LEARN.

"I don't know how" isn't a valid excuse for a dad. Sure, there are some things that are best left to the experts, but around the house chores are your responsibility. Killing spiders. Unclogging the drain. Dusting the ceiling fans. Washing windows. Cutting the grass. Your wife may insist on doing some things that a dad would normally do, but don't shirk your responsibility. And if you don't know how, LEARN. There isn't much you cannot find on YouTube these days. Take advantage of the digital age. Plus, you will have another arrow in your quiver to teach your kids.

Did you tell your wife you love her today?

June 28
DON'T GET TOSSED TODAY

Have you had a bad day at work? Are things not so comfy on the home front? Don't allow your bad day be the reason for unruly behavior at your child's game. There is a true story of an assistant basketball coach for a junior high team that showed up one day and told the head coach that "he was getting tossed today'. The head coach brushed it off as a joke. Then the game began. From the very start, the assistant coach was beligerant and before the end of the first half, he was thrown out of the game by the ref. His child was embarrassed. His wife was embarrassed. He made a fool of himself. He should have stayed home. Leave your problems at the gym door. Or better yet, don't attend at all if you cannot control your behavior. Don't get tossed today.

Did you tell your kids you love them today?

June 29

GO ON A PICNIC

It doesn't have to be far from your house, in fact, you can pretend in your backyard or balcony. The place doesn't matter. Pack a picnic lunch or dinner. Ask the kids to help. Let them pack their favorites even if they may not be the healthiest choices. If you can get to a bench in a park or find a picnic table, so much the better. Leave your phones behind. Kids sitting and dangling their feet at a picnic table will share whatever is on their mind. Maybe you can bring a book to read to them or have them bring a favorite book to share with the family. Tell them a story. Maybe it is about your grandfather they never met. Then have them tell a story. Before you know you have created a memory to be shared another day. You can bet they will ask you to do it again someday.

Did you tell your kids you love them today?

June 30

"GOOD TIRED"

There is a state that all of us can reach, but it easily falls upon parents more than others. It's called being 'good tired'. You probably have felt it even before I explain it. 'Good tired' is the feeling at the end of a day when little may have gone right for you. But you took care of your wife's car trouble. You sat with your son and helped him with his spelling homework. Your daughter wanted you to play soccer with her. All of this on top of the fact you worked ten hours today. You put your head on your pillow and asked yourself where the day had gone. And it hits you that tomorrow is going to be pretty much the same. But in spite of it all, you go to sleep with a sense of relief from a day well lived. Sleep tight my friend. You've earned it.

Whose day did you "make" today?

“Lord, when did we see you hungry or thirsty or a stranger or needing clothes or sick or in prison and did not help you?”

– MATTHEW 25:44

July 1

DO YOU KNOW YOUR NEIGHBOR?

Is your relationship with your neighbor confined to a passing, "Hello?" Have you ever simply sat down with your neighbor over coffee in the morning or for a beer in the backyard after work? In our lives, Our Lord places people in our lives for a reason. You live where you live for a reason. There are countless stories of people who were neighbors for years and never took the time to simply introduce themselves. Take the time. Chances are, you have a lot more in common with your neighbor than you think.

Whose day did you "make" today?

July 2

WHAT HAVE YOU GIVEN AWAY?

Is your home cluttered with stuff? How many coats does one man need? How many pairs of shoes do you need? One way to begin to unclutter your life is to practice what a priest related to me many years ago. If someone gives you a shirt, give one of your shirts away. If you buy a pair of pants, give one of your pairs of pants away. Get the picture? Only you control how cluttered your life is. Don't be surrounded by stuff. Give some of it away. If you let it, doing so will bring you a singular moment of peace. We can all use that.

Say a prayer today for one of the blessings in your life.

July 3
MAKE MEMORIES FOR OTHERS

It doesn't take a lot of effort, but you can help create a memory for someone else. Fewer and fewer of us are sending cards these days. The older you get, the more people in your life could use a boost, or a laugh or a note of encouragement. If you know someone who lost a job or someone whose parent died, send them a card or note. Conversely, if someone gets a new job or promotion or maybe gets a "hole in one," send them a note. Not only will they feel better, so will you.

Did you call or text a friend a message of hope today?

July 4

WHO WERE YOU MISTAKEN FOR TODAY

A priest was on vacation in Florida and he was on his daily walk on the beach when he noticed a man sheepishly approaching him. As the priest looked back at the man approaching, he saw a woman with two children cowering about fifty feet behind them. The man asked if the priest could spare a few dollars so that he might feed his family this morning. The priest looked around and saw there was a McDonalds just up the street from where they were and said, "I will not give you any money, but I will take your family to breakfast." The priest motioned for the woman and her son and daughter to catch up with them and they walked together to the Golden Arches. When they were getting ready to order, the priest encouraged them to order whatever they wanted. The children quickly ordered pancakes and sausage, while the parents both ordered a breakfast sandwich. While they were eating the priest found out more about the mother and father and the young son walked up to the table and asked if he could have more to eat. Before his father could respond, the priest said, "Certainly, order whatever you want." The boy looked up at the priest and said, "Are you God?" Who did you feed today? Who were you mistaken for today?

Whose day did you "make" today?

July 5

GIVE TO GOD WHAT IS GOD'S

Regardless of your faith, you have an obligation to render to the government what is the government's. As they say, nothing is more certain than death and taxes. But be sure that you render to God what is God's so that at your death it can be said of you that you gave your all. What is God's? Your money, your time and your prayer. Life doesn't have to be an equal amount of all three. It's your choice how to render to God what is God's. Spend wisely.

Whose day did you "make" today?

July 6

PSALM 112: 9

"He has distributed freely, he has given to the poor..."

Can this be said of you? Regardless of your state in life, someone is more in need than you. Have you given freely, lately? This is not a guilt trip. It is a reminder. Life has a few obligations. This is one of them. Whether it is the Thanksgiving season, the Christmas season or mid-August, you can always find somewhere to donate food, used or new clothing, or simply your time. In fact, time may be your most precious commodity. Giving your time brings personal contact with the children of God. Spend time with them and you will leave feeling better about yourself and whomever you helped. You will probably end up looking forward to the next opportunity to do the same.

Whose day did you "make" today?

July 7
BE THE FRIEND YOU WISH YOU HAD

Having trouble making friends? Maybe it's because you aren't being you. Maybe you need a new group of people to hang around with. (Easier said than done) The best way to get friends is to be the friend you wish you had. Don't 'sell out'. As stated earlier, there is only one you. People will gravitate to authentic people. Don't try to be somebody else. Be the friend you wish you had. Be you.

Did you call or text a friend a message of hope today?

July 8

WHO LENDS A HAND IN YOUR NEIGHBORHOOD?

No matter where you live, someone around you needs an occasional helping hand. Have your eyes and heart open to their needs. It can be as simple as taking out their trash cans when they are sick. If you live in the snow belt, clean off their windshield or maybe even shovel their sidewalk. Maybe they just need a few words with you. A simple hello. Get to know them so that when you recognize that something different is going on in their lives, you will know it. This is not being a 'busy body'. A busy body is just nosy. Be a neighbor who the other neighbors talk about for being there when needed. Someday, it may be their turn to help you

---

Whose day did you "make" today?

July 9

DON'T JUDGE

We can spend so much time looking at the faults of others that we lose sight of what really matters. Don't judge others. If you see faults in others, pray for them, or gently offer guidance if it is warranted/asked for. The only person you need to worry about going to hell is yourself. Life is too short to get so caught up in the faults of those around you. Live by example. Make your life shine so others will be attracted to you because of who you are. Don't judge, lest you be judged.

Did you call or text a friend a message of hope today?

July 10
THE WORLD IS TIRED OF CONFLICT

Common men want peace. Common men want to enjoy the solitude of a relationship with a wife and family. Common men want to work for a living and enjoy some time away with family and/or friends once in a while. The media wants to play with your mind and make you think that the world is a mess and it's your fault. They have to create conflict to make what they are spewing seem important. Love is important. Faith is important. Your daughter or son's questions are important. If we stopped worrying so much about what we don't have and gave thanks for what we do have, most contrived conflicts would vanish. Ignore the contrived conflict. Live a life that others wish they had. They will notice. Conflict will fade away. Love and faith will take its place. That's a great trade off, don't you think?

Say a prayer today for one of the blessings in your life.

July 11

WHAT ARE YOU CALLED TO DO?

If you have taken on the role of father, you automatically have the most important job of your life. Your relationship with your wife and children goes hand in hand. Get those two things right and you will be a success. You may be recognized at work for reaching sales goals or saving the company money or by being reliable and on time every day. That is all well and good and helps pay the bills. The best role you have doesn't pay much. Except in love, laughter and tears. Accept that form of pay and you will be rich forever.

Did you tell your wife you love her today?

July 12
BE YOU

Struggling with your place in the world? Feeling like your life needs a little spark? Too often, we can to look at the lives of others and think that they have it made. Nothing could be further from the truth. We can spend so much time trying to be somebody else that we forget to be ourselves. Look around your home. You have a wife that loves you. Children who love you. A roof over your head. Whether you know it or not, there are people looking at you thinking you have it made. Prove them right. Be you, everyone else is taken.

Say a prayer today for one of the blessings in your life.

July 13
HELP ALONG THE WAY

As a father and husband, you will from time to time find yourself with questions or issues that maybe you would rather not share with your father or mother. There may be good reason why someone outside of your family can provide guidance for you. Here's a tip for you. Try to find a mentor before you need one. Maybe someone at work. Maybe someone at church. Some of you may be lucky enough to have a neighbor who can fill the bill. Don't wait until you need help to go looking for it. Build some relationships now so that even if you never have a pressing issue or question, you will at least rest assured you know the help is there if you ever need it. Chances are, by having built these relationships, the answers will come to you simply by having known them.

Whose day did you "make" today?

July 14

CAN YOU SHARE YOUR FAITH OR NEED?

Do you have someone or someone's in your life that you can talk to when you are struggling. Some of you may have a brother or sister to call. Some of you can rely on a co-worker. Still, some may be involved with a small group where you worship. You don't know you need someone until you need someone. Sounds logical right? But do you? Life throws twists and turns at us. Some of which we may not have answers for. Reach out now, before you need to share a struggle. That way it will be easier when a twist or turn comes your way. You may be surprised that the person you reach out to may need you as well.

Did you call or text a friend a message of hope today?

July 15

LOOKING FOR LOVE IN ALL THE WRONG PLACES

For going on six decades, the number of abortions has continued to grow. Teenagers and young adults are having sex simply for the pleasure of it. Removing the traditional sense of love and goodness that had been associated with conjugal union for time immemorial. Teach your children that Love does not serve pleasure. Love serves goodness. The pleasure of the sexual union is sacred. Our world has taken too much away from us. Fight for what is good and sacred

---

Did you tell your kids you love them today?

July 16

TELL THE TRUTH

There is an old maxim: "Tell the truth, it's easier to remember." When confronted with situations that call for an explanation, the truth matters. It matters to you. It matters to your family. It matters to those you work with. The consequences are life changing. Living and telling the truth says everything about you. Your children will learn by what they see and follow suit. What better lesson could they possibly learn?

Did you tell your kids you love them today?

July 17
EXPLETIVE DELETED

The best way to delete expletives is to not use them in the first place. Sure, you probably have heard the words as far back as your early childhood but that is no excuse now that you have grown. Delete expletives from your language. Even among "the guys," don't use expletives. They only cast doubt on you and your character. Continued use of expletives could lead to you being deleted from those you want to be with. Only you can determine your fate among friends. Delete expletives so you don't find yourself deleted.

Did you call or text a friend a message of hope today?

July 18

YOUR MARITAL BOND

Marriage is a blending of two free spirits, yours and your wife's. During your courtship you found out a little about each other. When you "tie the knot" it becomes a whole new ballgame. Don't be surprised by seemingly strange habits or quirks your wife may have. Here's a bit of news for you...you have them too. Love is blending your free spirits to become one with each other. There may even be some conflict because of the quirks you discover. You will get over them. Remember, you promised to love and cherish each other the rest of your lives. Quirks and all.

Did you tell your wife you love her today?

July 19

TELL YOUR WIFE AND CHILDREN YOU ARE PROUD OF THEM

Recognition of effort is welcomed regardless of when it is received. Start telling your children you are proud of them for small achievements when they are young so that it will become a habit as they grow older. Tell your wife you are proud of the way she has helped you become the man you are. Besides your love, there may be no better gift they can receive from you. They will receive little praise from the outside world. Let them know how much they mean to you and they will hold their heads high. You will feel pretty good for having given the praise as well.

Did you tell your kids you love them today?

July 20

NO PRESSURE ON YOURSELF

Face it, not everyone is going to be financially secure. It is something to aspire to, but don't let it run your life. Do your best to provide a comfortable living for your wife and family. But don't let your drive for success blind you to what is important. If your wife tells you she loves you every day, that is success in itself. If your children tell you they love you every day, that is a double blessing. Put pressure on yourself to love your children and everything else will fall into place. No pressure, just love without measure.

Did you tell your wife you love her today?

July 21
A JOB WELL DONE

Making a house a home is not just a mother's job. Sure, your wife may decorate and organize the house to her own liking, but your attitude around the house can complete the décor. Don't bring work home with you. If you have had a bad day, don't take it out on your wife or children. Let them know you had a bad day, but don't ruin theirs. Let the love they will shower on you for your honesty seep in. You are her husband. You are their father. Those are your most important jobs. The earthly reward for being the best at those jobs is eternal. Quite a payment for a job well done.

Did you tell your kids you love them today?

July 22
FUN WITH KIDS

Have you gone swimming with your kids this summer? Did you run through a sprinkler or have a water balloon fight with them? Did you sit on your porch and eat a popsicle with them? Did you make some popcorn and sit and watch their favorite show? For your sake and theirs, make the answer to at least of couple of these ideas a "yes" before summer is over. Give them and you some simple memories to share years from now. They will remember what you did. They also will remember what you didn't do. Have some fun. Don't delay.

Did you tell your kids you love them today?

July 23
PARTICIPATION TROPHIES

Where do participation trophies end up a month or two after they are "awarded." Don't know the answer? You are not alone. The only person who likes participation trophies is the company that sells them. Kids know when recognition is deserved. They don't give out participation trophies for showing up to work on time. They don't give them when the oil needs to be changed in your car. Save recognition for when it is deserved. It will be appreciated all the more.

Whose day did you "make" today?

July 24

DID YOU SLEEP WELL LAST NIGHT?

How did you feel this morning when you woke up? Did you have a sleepless night? What may have been on your mind that kept you awake? Tonight, think to yourself: Did I do okay today? Not that you had to accomplish a lot, but who did you inspire today? Whose day did you make better? May I suggest that you add one word to the question. "Lord, did I do okay today?" If you honestly answer the question, you will either sleep well or toss and turn because of something you did or didn't do. Start a new habit tonight. If you have to, print the words and place them on your mirror or next to your bed. Then, before you fall asleep ask: "Lord, did I do okay today?" Do it often enough and soon you will sleep the sleep of the just, knowing He is your guide.

Say a prayer today for one of the blessings in your life.

July 25

CHRISTMAS IN JULY

It's five months until Christmas. Why not create a Christmas type memory for someone else...TODAY! It doesn't have to be anything big. The size is up to you. Send a card or letter to someone you know who could use a "pick me up." Make some cookies for your neighbor and drop them off, just because you can. Buy some food for the local food pantry. The gift is up to you. Celebrate life with others, just as you celebrate Christ's birth on Christmas. He will appreciate that you remembered what a gift that is.

Whose day did you "make" today?

July 26

RESPECT LAW ENFORCEMENT OFFICERS

The best way for you to teach your children to obey and respect law enforcement officers is to show them respect yourself. Children learn what they see. If you happen to pass a police officer on the street, stop and thank them for their service. If your children are with you, typically the officer will engage them in conversation. Show respect where respect is due and your children will learn to do the same.

Did you tell your kids you love them today?

July 27

READ A BOOK

When was the last time you read a book? Statistics show that fewer and fewer of us are reading, at all. Sure, we read messages on our phone. Or listen to YouTube videos. Or tune in to podcasts. But those only pique our interest for a few moments at a time. Discover or rediscover the treasure found in books. Our ancestors have left a lasting legacy of literary excellence. Revel in it. You may not like the first book you pick up. Ask a friend or work colleague if they have read a good book recently. Then, once you have found a good book, share it with someone else. It will create a connection that you didn't know existed. Then, find another good book and start the cycle again.

Did you call or text a friend a message of hope today?

July 28

FOOD AND FUN CAN CREATE SUSTAINING MEMORIES

Every family has a list of foods or fun activities that span through the years. Simple activities that remind us we are children at heart. Desserts that only a mom could make. Tossing water balloons with each other. Driving to get soft-serve ice cream when it is scorching hot outside. Spraying whipped cream into your child's or grandchildren's mouth until it over flows. The chocolate cake that only grandma made just so. A relish tray on Christmas that no one eats. Every family has these memories. Keep the old ones alive and create new ones. The memories will last for generations.

Did you tell your kids you love them today?

July 29

WHO IS THERE TO MOURN

Watch the evening news or read the local paper online. Whenever there is a young man killed or wounded in a shooting, rarely do you hear or read a quote from the father. You will hear from the mother, or grandmother or aunt or the neighbor lady next door. Where is the father? Where is dad? Increasingly, the absence of fathers in young men's lives has become a national crisis. This hasn't happened overnight. Why as a society do we continue to ignore the necessity for a father to be there for his children? Sadly, this is not another occasion of painting with abroad brush. Be there to watch your children grow. Help your son become a man. Otherwise, he will tend to look elsewhere for attention.

Did you tell your kids you love them today?

July 30

RESPECT YOUR CHILDREN

Your children are your children. But don't be their friend. There is a fine line between being a parent and being a friend. Don't let your love for them breakdown your parental responsibility. Set limits. This doesn't mean you can't have fun with them. It means just the opposite. Nurture the love for your children by being part of their lives. Limits show how much you love them. Just ask kids whose parents haven't set limits. Look how they are struggling. Be a parent first. That is the respect your children deserve.

Did you tell your kids you love them today?

July 31

THERE IS STILL TIME

Even at the end of July, you still have time for some summer fun. Within reason, try to leave nothing undone. Next year your children will be a year older and the activities they will want to do will be different from this year's. Don't find yourself wishing you had done this or that. If you made plans, see them through. Time spent with family is never wasted. Time not spent with family can be wasted. And you cannot get that time back. You don't have to be Clark Griswold, trying to cram a summer of fun into a week. Use the time you have left this summer to create some new memories. They will be priceless and may become part of Thanksgiving Day lore in the future.

Did you tell your wife you love her today?

"If you want to bring happiness to the whole world, go home and love your family."

– ST. MOTHER TERESA

August 1
YOUR ESCAPE PLAN

We have all been there. You have had a bad day at work. Or the news of the day has gotten you down. Maybe you find yourself with a group of guys you would rather not be around. You hear a story of a co-worker that has just left his wife. On days like this, follow the wisdom of St. Mother Theresa of Calcutta: "If you want to bring happiness to the whole world, go home and love your family." Hopefully you won't have to do this often, but imagine if on a given day one percent of the world did this. And then another one percent does it tomorrow. And so on and so on. How much better off would we all be?

Did you tell your wife you love her today?

August 2
MOST IMPORTANT THING IN THEIR LIVES

What's the most important thing in your child's life? You! Ask any child who doesn't have a mother or father in their lives, what they want most and the answer will come down to having parents. It's easy to spot the kids that don't, just as it is easy to spot the kids that do. Be sure your kids do. It's the toughest job you will ever do. But it's not cliché' to say it is your most rewarding job. Be the most important thing in their lives. Give all of yourself to your children every day of their lives. It is rare that this attention goes unrewarded. What will be most glaring is if you don't give them attention. They will look for it elsewhere. Imagine where that might lead.

Did you tell your kids you love them today?

August 3

NAMES MEANS SOMETHING

When you are choosing names for your children follow one simple rule: That child will have to live with that name for the rest of their lives. They may be subject to jokes and taunting because you and/or your wife wanted something "different." It is a parent's prerogative to name their children. Don't take that job lightly. You are sure to have heard what you thought were strange names for children in the past. Don't add your child to the list. Names mean something. Take one of the most important jobs a parent has seriously. Your child will thank you for it.

Did you tell your kids you love them today?

August 4

TELL HER SHE'S CUTE

She is your best friend. She bore your children. She thinks you are handsome. She may even like your singing voice. When was the last time you told her she was cute? Did you compliment her on her shoes the last time she got dressed up when you went out? Did you ever thank her for letting you watch "The Shawshank Redemption" (insert your favorite movie title here) for the twentieth time? You won't remember every day but occasionally insert a compliment to your wife just because she loves you more than anything else in life. What more reason do you need?

Did you tell your wife you love her today?

August 5
HOLD THEM TIGHT

Life can throw many challenges at us in our walk on this earth. It is how we prepare for these challenges that help us bear adversity. One of the best ways to prepare is to get in the habit of hugging your wife and your children. Tightly. Do it over and over again. So that when the time comes when words aren't enough, they will know you care.

Did you tell your wife you love her today?

August 6

DEALING WITH FAILURE

Losing sucks. Plain and simple. But dealing with losing separates "the men from the boys." We are not just talking about sports. There will be everyday situations when your child may lose. How they recover from a loss will determine future success. Don't make huge deals over victories. Don't make huge deals over losses. Well-rounded children know how to handle winning and losing. Help them, especially when they over emphasize either result.

Did you tell your kids you love them today?

August 7
THE OLD WAY AIN'T NECESSARILY BAD

If you are a parent, you have also been someone's child. And you probably heard yourself say to your parents: "That's the old way of doing things." Now that you are a parent, you will inevitably hear the same in so many words. Stand tall and defend the past. The old way isn't necessarily bad. We ignore the old way at our own peril. Don't be blind to change, but don't let someone tell you that you are intolerant, when by saying so, they are being intolerant as well. Listen to each other. Be open to change. Sometimes they will have to see the mistake of their own ways until they realize that in some cases, THE OLD WAY AIN'T NECESSARILY ALL BAD.

Did you tell your kids you love them today?

August 8

DID YOU LISTEN

Who are your faith role models? Typically, we learn our faith from our parents and/or grandparents. Maybe you had a teacher or neighbor who guided you along your faith journey. Rest assured that God had a hand in that development. All of us, no matter how shallow or deep our faith currently is, have had someone that Our Lord has placed in our lives to provide guidance. Too often, however, we ignore that guidance. We turn our backs to those who can assist in our walk with Our Lord. Take a few moments to look back at your faith journey. Did you listen or did you ignore the guidance? How different would your life be had you taken to heart guidance offered in the past?

Whose day did you "make" today?

August 9

WHERE HAVE ALL THE FATHERS GONE?

What happened? In the course of the last fifty years, the role of the father in our modern society has dwindled to a flicker of a flame. Look around you to see the evidence. Increased street violence. Increased drug use. Increased dropout rates. The effects of the abdication of men regarding their role as fathers has brought us to a tipping point. Look at who is quoted when a young man is taken before his time. All too often, we hear about a grieving mother, grandmother or aunt. Rarely is there a mention of a father. How many athletes do we hear about that have multiple children with multiple "baby mommas?" Who is going to step up and say "enough is enough?"

Did you tell your kids you love them today?

August 10

ENCOURAGE YOUR CHILDREN TO GET INVOLVED

Active children are happier children. Children who sit at home in front of a TV or computer screen as their free time activity will be susceptible to behaviors that can easily lead them astray. Active children who participate in sports or the arts or volunteer activities, just to name a few, will be happier and probably healthier. Yes, you will have to take them to and/or pick them up from these activities but it will be time well spent for both of you. Heck, maybe you can even engage in a conversation with them without using a phone. Imagine that!

Did you tell your kids you love them today?

August 11

FEAST OF ST. CLARE OF ASSISI

St. Clare was of noble birth. She was attracted to the simple life she saw St. Francis living and gave up her earthly comforts to answer a call to serve. Her father and uncle tried in vain to convince her to return to her former way of life. She chose to serve the poor and neglected just like St. Francis. The order of religious women she started, The Poor Clares of Perpetual Adoration, has thousands of sisters around the world. Clare and so many like her who gave up everything to answer the call to serve, provide the ultimate example of mimicking Christ's call to serve. Listen for your call. It may not reach around the world like Francis and Clare. Maybe just reaching across the street can be your call. Neither Francis or Clare knew how far their love would spread. Nor do you. Reach out, see how far your reach can spread.

Whose day did you "make" today?

August 12

SOMETIMES, LOVE ISN'T ENOUGH

It may not become part of your experience and for that you can be eternally grateful, but you may know or have heard of situations in a family's life when love just isn't enough. The horror of drug addiction or mental illness or mind games played by domineering personalities can attract children from even the best of families. Despite heartfelt and utterly sincere efforts of family and friends, children may be led astray. At some point, you simply have to let go. It doesn't mean your stop loving them or praying for them. It is one of life's cruel tricks. No one said raising children was easy. Hug 'em every chance you get. But sometimes, love just isn't enough.

Did you tell your kids you love them today?

August 13

MIRACLES HAPPEN

You woke up today. Your children are healthy. Most of the bills are paid. Your wife just gave you a kiss as she whisked the kids out the door for school. These are all gifts, signs of the daily miracles of life. Not all miracles are made into movies. Celebrate the day-to-day gifts in your life.

Say a prayer today for one of the blessings in your life.

August 14

AVERAGE AIN'T BAD

Not every kid can get straight A's. Most kids don't get straight A's. Average is not something you shoot for but it might be what your child achieves. Maybe that is the best he or she can do. Watch the effort they put in. If your child spends more than ample time on his or her studies, accept the results. If there is a lack of effort then a conversation may be in order. Help your child along the way. Be proud of what they achieve. Reward effort. Average ain't bad.

Did you tell your kids you love them today?

August 15

LOOK FOR A ROLE MODEL

If your experience with fatherhood has not been a pleasant memory you have a choice to make. Either you can be bitter about not having a dad, which is somewhat justified, or you can look around and find a role model from whom you can learn the finer points of fatherhood. The choice is yours. A simple first step is to commit to loving your wife and children. Giving your whole self to them, warts and all, will be appreciated more than you can imagine. You are going to make mistakes. Just don't make big ones. You probably know someone at work or where you worship or maybe a neighbor who seems to "have it together" as a father. Your wife and children will let you know when you screw up. Just admit it and move on. Better off for having tried and failed than not to have tried at all.

Did you tell your wife you love her today?

August 16

WE DON'T KNOW HOW TO COMMUNICATE

Do you and your children bring a phone to the dinner table? Do you sit around the house starring at your phone? Does your wife do the same? Unfortunately, for many homes, the answer to the above questions is Yes, Yes, and Yes. And yet, you probably complain that your kids don't talk to you. How can they when they can't get your attention. And we wonder why children can't communicate not only with parents but with others as well. They learn what they see. Our "depersonalized" society is a result of our supposed "connectedness." Connected to what? A cell phone and/or computer connects us to things. Conversations connect us to each other. Limit cell phone and computer use in your home. Learn to communicate the old-fashioned way. It has worked since man began to grunt with each other. It can still work today.

Did you tell your kids you love them today?

August 17
LEAVE YOUR PHONE IN THE CAR

When you go to a restaurant with your wife and or family, do you take your phone with you? (When you have time to go to a restaurant.) It seems that no matter where you go today, people sit and stare at their phones instead of connecting with each other. Why go out at all if you are allowing distractions to get in the way? Leave your phone in the car, or at least on silent, but don't use it while you are spending time with your wife or loved ones. Family connections lead to family memories. It is amazing what you can find out from your children if you are engaged with them. The reward for doing so is priceless.

Did you tell your kids you love them today?

August 18

CAN'T MAKE THE HURT GO AWAY

There are some of our fellow men and women who have faced hurt and rejection that only they can feel. We are helpless to soothe the pain. Seemingly, all we can do is be there for them to share a hug or lend an ear to the latest spark that fueled the release of the memory from the recesses of their personal vault. They hoped would never be reopened. Maybe the hurt will never go away. I recall a scene from the movie "Forrest Gump." Forrest's friend Jenny has run away from her past for most of her life. Never being able to run far enough to lose that deeply imbedded memory. Jenny and Forrest are on a walk and they pass the home that Jenny grew up in and she begins to throw stones at the abandoned house. Hurling stone after stone until she falls to the ground in tears. Forrest is narrating at this point in the movie, not speaking to her. He states, "Sometimes there just aren't enough stones." When confronted with such emotions we want to solve the unsolvable. Sometimes, we can only hand them more stones to throw.

Did you call or text a friend a message of hope today?

August 19
EAT ICE CREAM

Life is too short to not have a few pleasures once in a while. Whether it be ice cream or a piece of cake or a good piece of chocolate, stop and enjoy the simple pleasures. Better yet, do it with your wife and family. Simple pleasures give us a moment to stop and enjoy each other. Have you ever sat and watched your kids eat ice cream? They will be lost in conversation with each other. They will giggle and mix-up the toppings into what doesn't look like ice cream anymore. So what? Enjoy the simple pleasures. They will remember the simple stuff as they grow older and will pass the simple on to their children. Not any harm in that, is there?

Did you tell your kids you love them today?

August 20

ENJOY THE SIMPLE THINGS

Surely, you can buy a 16-ounce porterhouse and an expensive bottle of wine, followed by an expensive cigar. It is good to treat yourself sometimes. But don't forget the simpler things. A hot dog with horseradish and relish. A bacon, lettuce and tomato sandwich. A sparkling glass of iced tea on your back porch. Watching you children play in the park. Your life is full of a never-ending supply of the simpler things. Enjoy the simple things.

Say a prayer today for one of the blessings in your life.

August 21

WHAT KEEPS YOU FROM WHAT YOU LOVE

Sure, we all have plans and as they say "Life gets in the way." But don't allow distractions to keep you from what you love. The time to do what you love is now. Plan to spend time with your wife. Plan to spend time with your kids. Plan a moment or two for yourself once in a while. Believe it or not, the devil wants to get in your way. Be aware of the distractions that keep you from what you are doing. Yes, work does get in the way, but don't be a workaholic. Chores around the house will get in the way, but you can trim the bushes tomorrow. Don't let distractions keep you from what you love.

Did you tell your kids you love them today?

August 22

TRAPPED OR FREE?

Think of the happiest people you know. What kind of life do they live? Chances are they have time for others. Chances are they exercise regularly. Chances are they have little worry about debt. Chances are they find time to play with their kids after dinner. Do you have time for others? When was the last time you took a walk with your wife? Is credit debt piling up? Trapped or free? It's your choice. If trapped, don't try to get "free" overnight. You didn't trap yourself in the past month. Recognizing you are trapped is your first step to feeling free. Take that first step. The next step will be even easier.

Whose day did you "make" today.

August 23

ADOPTING, FOSTERING OR MENTORING CHILDREN

There is no greater gift you can give a child than to welcome them into your home or being there for them during their formative years. It is only common sense. Children who are loved and nurtured are going to have a leg up on those who are not. Look at your life. Look at your family. Is there room for one more? Is their quality time for one more? Can you spare a few hours a week to mentor a child? The rewards are priceless. Don't delay. Speak with your wife about taking this step in your lives. It is not for everyone, but maybe it is meant for you.

Whose day did you "make" today.

August 24
A HONEYMOON CONTRACT

Thinking about how your relationship with your wife will continue over the years will be the subject of conversation from time to time. It can lead to some funny results. On our wedding night, my wife and I decided that we would have a sixty-four year trial period before we signed a binding contract to stay married. It provided a laugh then and it continues to provide a laugh to this day. You need to interject some levity into your married life. It will help you get through the days that seem to run together from time to time. Find your own story lines. Have fun with your relationship.

Did you tell your wife you love her today?

August 25
DANCE LIKE NO ONE IS WATCHING

Have you ever gone to a wedding or outdoor summer concert and seen people dancing like they haven't a care in the world? You look at them and decide you are going to skip the dancing. Or, you tell yourself you could never sing like that. Here's a hint: loosen up a little. No one will remember tomorrow if they saw you dancing. No one will remember you couldn't carry a tune in a bucket. In fact, maybe they look at you and wonder why you aren't dancing or singing. Dance like no one is watching. Sing like no one is listening. Because they aren't.

Whose day did you "make" today?

August 26

STICK TO YOUR GUNS!

It may be an old-fashioned use of words, but what better way to describe the role of a father and mother. Your kids need rules. Your kids want rules. There are examples all around us of kids that act out because they don't know the rules. Sure, your kids will push back at times, but they will understand your love for them by how you want to protect them. They are not old enough to decide for themselves. You and your wife need to be their shining light. Don't hide it under a basket. Let them know and hear the rules of the house.

Did you tell your kids you love them today?

August 27

MR. FIXIT

Your drain is clogged, or your disposal is stuck. You can spend hour upon hour frustrating yourself trying to unclog the drain or fixing the disposal. Face it. You can't fix everything. Sure, we all know a guy who can fix anything. But unless he is your next-door neighbor, break down and call somebody. Chances are the cost to fix the original problem will be less than the damage you caused by trying to fix it yourself. Don't learn the hard way. Let someone else take care of what you don't know. It's always cheaper in the long run. Besides, you might miss your child's soccer game or your favorite show on TV by trying to be Mr. Fix It.

Did you tell your kids you love them today?

August 28

VOLUNTEER…COACH…TEACH

You don't have to wait to be a father to start being involved in other children's lives. There are countless opportunities to volunteer, mentor, coach or teach children. In fact, some men are better doing these things apart from their family. There is nothing wrong with that. You may want to have other adults coaching or teaching your children. Either way, be the best you can be for those you encounter. Don't bring your frustrations from work or family into your volunteering. If you have had a bad day and cannot leave the bad day behind, don't volunteer that day. No one will think the worst of you. They will respect your honesty. Be at your best when lending a helping hand so that those you encounter will learn to be their best.

Did you tell your kids you love them today?

August 29

HAS IT BEEN A LONG WEEK?

Does it seem like the weekend will never get here? Feeling like a gerbil on a treadmill? Make plans to change things up this weekend. If you normally get right out of bed on Saturday morning, roll over and sleep in. If your wife is the one who had the long week, get out of bed and tend to the kids. Let her "sleep" in. Changing a routine will make the weekend seem different. Different is good. Treat yourself to different so you are ready for the next long week that starts on Monday. Monday will come soon enough. Be sure you are ready.

Did you tell your wife you love her today?

August 30

WASTED LIVES

Their stories are handed down from generation to generation. Families are reminded of "the bad seed" in the family that either died too soon or left an indelible black mark on their family. The result of their wasted lives should be a warning to us. We worship rock stars and "celebrities" only to find out how dark their lives were. The list is seemingly endless: Hendrix, Joplin, Morrison, Cass, Bonham, Belushi, Farley, etc. Don't let those in your life fall into a downward cycle that ruins not only their life but those around them. Life is too short to be wasted. Celebrate it.

Whose day did you "make" today?

August 31

ULTIMATE RESPONSIBILITY

Each of us is ultimately responsible for the life we live. Don't use your surroundings as an excuse for your behavior. Look at the example of Jesus. He told us the kingdom of God is here. The life we live is not judged by man. It is only in the final judgement that our actions are brought to light. Will your actions save or doom you? If we live the Kingdom of God on earth, our judgements will save us. It is your choice.

Say a prayer today for one of the blessings in your life.

"Shalom, Shalom."

September 1
SHALOM, SHALOM.

In ancient times, the Jewish people would greet each other by saying, "Shalom." It simply means peace. Extended meanings include harmony and wholeness. It also was used whether you were first meeting someone or saying goodbye. It worked both ways. Interestingly, if you said it twice it is said to mean "perfect peace." What better way to greet a family member, or a neighbor, or anyone who comes into your life today. Seems like we could all use some perfect peace, don't you think? "Shalom, shalom." Pass it on.

Whose day did you "make" today?

September 2

A DAILY HUG

We all need assurance on a daily basis. The best assurance you can give your wife is to hold her in your arms at least once a day. Sounds fairly simple, but in our busy world, easily forgotten. On some days, this may be the only moment of peace in either of your days. It wouldn't be a bad idea to try to have this moment with each of your children as well. Enjoy the peace.

Did you tell your wife you love her today?

September 3
A LIVING AND GROWING SYSTEM

Family life revolves around interpersonal relationships. Your relationship with your oldest child will be different from your relationship with your youngest child. It is not intentional, it is just how life works. No two of us are the same. As families grow and interact, sharing joys and sorrows, each member's experience allows them to have an individual perspective. Dealing with this variety of perspectives gives life its flavor. Savor the flavor. Otherwise, life can get awfully bland.

Did you tell your kids you love them today?

September 4

DO NOT RUN AWAY

No one begs you to be a father. Just like no one begs you to be a particular religion. If they do, run away. Becoming a father is a life choice that should happen after realizing that you are ready to accept the awesome responsibility to help, not only bring a life into the world, but to mold it, play with it and ultimately love it more than life itself. Once you have made the choice, you cannot run from the responsibility. Embrace it. The rewards are endless.

Did you tell your kids you love them today?

September 5

NOW

Do you really need a watch? Are you too pre-occupied with time? Sure, you have to be on-time for work. You have to get the kids ready for school on-time. But as you go about your "everyday," teach yourself to live "in the moment." You can get so caught up in what happened yesterday. Or, you can spend a lot of time worrying about tomorrow, when the present moment is all that matters. There was an old NFL coach who had all of the clocks in the locker changed so that instead of numbers, there was the word, "NOW" in twelve positions around the clock. Teach yourself to live "in the NOW." And watch what a change it can bring,

---

Whose day did you "make" today?

September 6

WRITE A LETTER TO SOMEONE TODAY

Millennials, and those younger among us, may not know how to communicate one-on-one. Of course, they text or "connect" on Instagram or Twitter. But real interpersonal communication is lacking. And at the same time, we are no longer teaching children how to write cursive. Want to totally surprise someone? Write a personal letter. Find a piece of paper, a pen, an envelope and a stamp. Sit down and tell someone how special they are. Tell them why you chose to write the letter. They will have to open the letter and sit down and read it. Then, challenge them to pick someone they know to write a letter to. This could bring a whole new meaning to chain letters.

Whose day did you "make" today?

September 7
GRACE

Have you ever heard someone say: "There but for the grace of God go I?" Ever heard yourself say it? To some, grace is the toughest word for them to define. Whether you can define it or not, it is all around you. It comes from above. And it is FREE! Like all great things in life, it comes with no strings attached. You just have to accept it. Not sure where to find grace? Did you wake up this morning? Did your wife kiss you when you left for or came home from work? Did your children leave for school today clothed and nourished? Looks like you are surrounded by Grace! ENJOY!

Say a prayer today for one of the blessings in your life.

September 8
IT'S FALL

Summer is over, the kids are in school, but the fun doesn't have to stop. The possibilities are endless for family fun in the autumn of the year. Trails are more fun when it isn't blazing hot outside. Campfires can be a source of laughter and good food. And, there is always pumpkin-spiced something readily available. Encourage your kids to come up with some suggestions for family fun. Create lasting memories that they and you will want to repeat year after year.

Did you tell your kids you love them today?

September 9

"I LOVE YOU, TOO"

Something that I have noticed in recent years is the number of people who are on their phone with their spouse or one of their children and at the end of the conversation you hear them say, "I love you," or "I love you, too." Part of this is because we have cell phones in our hands or nearby throughout the day and our conversations may not be as private as they once were. But it is refreshing to hear anyway. It says something about you when someone hears you say "I love you." Not only to whom the words are directed, but to those who hear them indirectly. Soon, you may hear a co-worker or friend end their conversation with an "I love you," because they heard it from you. That's a gift that keeps on giving.

Did you tell your wife you love her today?

September 10

MAKE A FRIEND

It is said that most of us are lucky if we have one or two good friends. How many friends to you have. Not just acquaintances, but somebody you can confide in. If you were in dire need of speaking to someone about your faith or the loss of a loved one or that you hate your job, whom would you turn to? If the answer is no one, then maybe the problem is you. Have you ever lent an ear to a friend or coworker in their time of need? Did you ever hug a guy because you knew he was hurting? You don't need a reason. Make a friend. Make another. Join a small group at your church. Or, find someone at work that you relate to. Chances are they need someone like you to step out for them. Then, when you need a hug or someone to listen to you, you won't have to go far to find them.

Did you call or text a friend a message of hope today?

September 11
KEEP THOSE SAPPY CARDS

You just celebrated a birthday, or Father's Day or your anniversary or someone close to you passed away. Someone or someone's gave you a card. What did you do with the card(s)? I would like to encourage you to keep them. There was a reason you were given those cards. You may not appreciate it today, but years from now you may. I have a stack in my dresser that is over an inch thick of old cards. Old cards, but never ending sentiments of love and support. Keepers, in my book.

Say a prayer today for one of the blessings in your life.

September 12

FORGIVENESS IS A GIFT

Are you carrying a burden with you because you haven't found the courage to ask someone for forgiveness? You might be surprised not only how much better the person you are asking may feel, but how much better you will feel. We all carry burdens. Some are heavier than others. But only we have the power to empty ourselves of those burdens. Chances are both of you will feel so much better and your relationship may take a direction that neither of you saw as possible. Forgiveness is a gift, both for the giver and receiver. Cherish that gift.

Whose day did you "make" today?

September 13
ONE PURPOSE

The role of parents is vast. Lots of responsibilities, along with lots of fun and laughter. Lots of tears, both of sorrow and joy. At the root of it all is your most precious duty: To get your children to heaven. How much of your time and effort you spend in fulfilling this duty is up to you. It's a daily responsibility. Your children will be aware of your efforts because they are at the root of all you do. Your daily coming and going. Your daily expression of love for your wife and children. How you treat those who you come into contact with on a daily basis will influence how your children perceive your actions. All leading to the way they treat those they encounter which impacts their own journey to heaven. Lead the way.

Did you tell your kids you love them today?

September 14

GOD'S PLAN FOR EACH SOUL

What have we lost over the centuries due to war or tyrannical behavior or abortion? What have we lost because mankind has killed or abandoned countless millions of souls? What songs have been left unwritten? What cures have never been discovered? How much loneliness have we created by living our own life instead of welcoming new life? How much laughter has been lost? How much love has been lost? Let's let God do the planning and He will leave the living to us.

Did you tell your kids you love them today?

September 15

DON'T MISS IT

Your never get a second chance to see something happen for the first time. The first soccer goal. The first dance recital. The first home run. The first "A" on a report card. Remember when you were a kid? These important moments in life are made all the more special because your mother and/or father were there to celebrate it. Sure, the goal was his or her first, but if you were there, you will never forget how it felt. Don't rob your kids of these memories. Celebrate life's precious moments.

Did you tell your kids you love them today?

September 16

THE JONES MAY WISH THEY WERE YOU

"Keeping up with the Jones'" is a pre-occupation of many people. Striving to have what they have and go where they go can take your eye off what's most important. Have you ever thought how much time and effort it takes the Jones' to keep up with what they have? Are you willing to put in the hours it takes to have what they have? Did it ever occur to you that the Jones' may be slightly envious of you? It's okay to want "things" for your wife and children. Just don't let "things" get in the way of living a life that is a model for even the Jones.'

Say a prayer today for one of the blessings in your life.

September 17
TIME TO DO SO

What is it you love to do but have little time to do? What is it your wife loves to do but has little time to do? The older you get, the more you may find yourself saying: "I wish I'd had more time to do that when I was younger." Take it from anyone you may encounter who is in their golden years. They can probably share a regret for having let time pass them by. From time to time, have discussions with your wife about what she would like to do if she just had the time. Share what you would like to do as well. Then, find the time to do so. Don't wait until you are in your golden years and you are asked the question. Find time to do so. Then your answer will not be: "I wish I had." Your answer will be: "This is what I did...."

Did you tell your wife you love her today?

September 18

A DAILY GIFT OF 24 HOURS

Each new day is a gift of 24 hours. Nobody gets more, nobody gets less. What defines you is how you use your daily gift. You don't have to put yourself on a schedule but each day should include: time spent in prayer, time spent with your children and time spent with your wife. Of course, you have to allow time for work, but don't allow your commitment at work detract from your responsibilities at home. Successful families make sure they have quality time together. How you make use of your time will directly influence the lives of those around you. And yes, it is okay to carve a few moments each day for you. Keep an eye on what's important and you deserve those few moments for yourself.

Whose day did you "make" today?

September 19

WE SHOULD GRIEVE TOGETHER

Families that do everything together are becoming rarer every day. There are too many distractions that keep us apart. If you laugh together, you will cry together. If you celebrate birthdays together, your children will experience love. Most importantly, we must grieve together. Not one of us should grieve alone. We need each other, even if all you offer is a sincere hug. The words we offer to those grieving come very hard. But it is not the words that matter, it is your presence that counts. Grieve together.

Say a prayer today for one of the blessings in your life.

September 20

THE PAST IS PAST

No matter how old you are you have a past that you either want to forget or hold dear. Regardless of your past, don't let it define your future. Learn from the past but don't wallow in it. You determine your future. Don't let it be darkened by what has happened. Let it shine brightly because of how you live in the present. Shine on...

Whose day did you "make" today?

September 21

BE THERE NOW

What brings your child happiness? Whether it be singing or drawing or playing a sport, show you care by showing interest in what they do. Don't allow yourself to have excuses for not being involved. Sure, your work schedule may get in the way and for that your kids will understand. But, aside from work, be sure their interests are more important than yours. Their success in life depends on you BEING THERE. Don't end up in your later years wishing you had been there for your kids. Be there now.

Did you tell your kids you love them today?

September 22

DO YOU READ TO YOUR CHILDREN?

Most mothers love to read to their children. There is an innate ability for a mother to relate this way. Dads can do it too! Take the time to read to your children. If nothing else, it will allow you to sit and relax for a few precious moments that you will never get back. Bring the book to life. Be silly. Make faces. Raise your voice as necessary. Be a kid reading to a kid. Your children will never forget it. Dr. Suess is a great start and probably not a bad place to finish. I bet that if you read to your kids, when they become parents, they will do the same. In fact, I am sure of it.

Did you tell your kids you love them today?

September 23
STRONG CONFIDENT CHILDREN

Did you tell your child (children) that you are proud of them today? Praise can be for the simplest things: Saying thank you, saying you're welcome, picking up their toys, finishing homework, etc. Letting your kids know that you are proud of them builds confidence. It builds self-respect. They will walk taller because of it. Praise is so lacking in our lives. We take so much for granted and forget to acknowledge the efforts of others. If your children are older and maybe out of your house, tell them how proud you are for the adult they have become. Before you know it, your children whatever their age, will treat those around them the same way.

Did you tell your kids you love them today?

September 24

IT'S BECAUSE OF CONFIDENCE

If you build your child's confidence, the results will be reaped for years to come. Do your children like sports or reading or the fine arts? Whatever their interest is, acknowledge how much it means to them by backing them up with praise. Even when they fall short of their own goals acknowledge their effort. Teach them that it is in the trying that they get better. Acknowledge incremental steps of improvement, however small the steps may be, and watch their confidence grow. Not everyone can be a winner. But being on the team or finishing a difficult book or being part of a chorus at school shows they want to improve. Make sure they know you recognize and appreciate their effort.

Did you tell your kids you love them today?

September 25
NO PRESSURE

It is your duty to be sure that the pressures of life don't wear on your children. Teaching them from a young age to learn from failure as opposed to letting failure "haunt" them will set them up for success later in life. Be sure there are equal parts of fun in their lives. They will all too soon grow up and face the "work a day" world. Having fun along the way will mold them into adults who know how to accept what life throws at them Don't pressure them to succeed. Teach them the joys of a life well lived.

Did you tell your kids you love them today?

September 26

YOUR STRESS LEVEL IS THEIR STRESS LEVEL

We have discussed previously how children will mimic your actions. They will pick up repeated behavior. If you are stressed out on a regular basis, they will be stressed out also. Do them and yourself a favor, leave the stress at the door. It doesn't mean you forget about it, but don't bring it home. Save the discussions for private time with your spouse. Your wife will know you are stressed. She bought into life's good and bad when she married you. Give your kids a pass on stress. They are having a hard enough time just being kids.

Did you tell your kids you love them today?

September 27
RESPECT THE WORK OF YOUR WIFE

Our wives can wear many hats, sometimes two or three on a daily basis. They probably start the day in the role of mother. Then, they may either work or volunteer during the day. And, hopefully, they have time to spend with you at some point during waking hours. Regardless of the hats she has worn, make sure your wife knows that you respect the roles she plays in your children's lives, those she encounters on a daily basis and yours. Let her know the gift she is to you. Chances are pretty good she will tell you the same.

Did you tell your wife you love her today?

September 28

CAREFREE TIMELESSNESS

It you are not in the habit of doing so, treat yourself to regular helpings of carefree timelessness. A walk in the cool morning air. Driving with your windows open and no radio on for distraction. Sit outside at night and just look at the sky. Carefree timelessness allows the mind to unwind. It doesn't cost you a dime. The reward is beyond measure.

Say a prayer today for one of the blessings in your life.

September 29
GROW INTO IT

Just as an oversized article of clothing can be grown into, so can accepted behavior. Children grow out of clothing. They should not grow out of accepted behavior. Praising them when they exhibit behaviors that may even surprise you can go a long way. Let them know when you are proud of the way they treat others. Let them know when you see them respect their elders. Your recognition will be remembered and repeated as a result. Then watch them grow into adults that others will want to be around.

Did you tell your kids you love them today?

September 30

17 INCHES

I encourage you to look up the following. Just type "17 inches John Scolinos" in the search bar on your computer screen. Take time to watch the entire video. Sure, it may seem like old-school teaching, but it remains true today. We are widening the plate. Anyone who knows the game of baseball will tell you that widening of the plate is not a good thing. When rules are not followed, do you hold your children accountable or do you "widen the plate?" Think what would happen to you at work if you told your boss that you were only going to work thirty-two hours a week and yet expect forty hours of pay. Or, how do you explain to a policeman writing you a ticket that you thought you could drive 75 in a 55 zone? You widen the plate at the expense of your children. Let your children know the rules and don't widen the plate. They will thank you for it when they are older.

Did you tell your kids you love them today?

"I would rather be a builder than a wrecker, hoping always that the structure of life is growing—not dying."

– FRANKLIN DELANO ROOSEVELT

October 1

CELEBRATE THE "EVERY DAY"

Don't have such high expectations that every day is going to work out just the way you want it. Most days are simply normal days. Celebrate normal. Yes, it can even seem boring at times. Tedious. Nerve racking. Insert your own description. Guess what? You are not alone. As they say, "Rome wasn't built in a day." Be patient. Be loving. Be present. Then watch the magic of your loving touch mold your children into something you never imagined. It won't happen overnight. Celebrate the every day. Big things are around the corner.

Say a prayer today for one of the blessings in your life.

October 2

WE COMPLICATE THINGS

Why does your life seem so busy? Do you wake up in the morning already certain that today is just another in a series of comings and goings? Sure, you have a lot to do today. But, make today different from yesterday. Uncomplicate things. Grab a few moments in the morning, even if it means getting up earlier, just to be together. You don't even have to get out of bed. You will feel better for it. Take charge of your daily existence. We complicate things by anticipating what every day is going to bring. Bring a little more of those you love into special moments in your life. Life will suddenly seem simpler.

Did you call or text a friend a message of hope today?

October 3

ANOTHER SAD STATISTIC

"Over 95% of the worst drug users never had a solid father figure in their life." That is a quote from the founder of the "home of last resort" for drug offenders in Cincinnati, Ohio. Kind of makes sense, doesn't it? Kids with a solid father figure may stray from time to time, but because of the influence a father has, they seldom stray far. They will test limits but only go so far. Good dads teach character. Heck, even a bad father can instill a sense of right or wrong with his child. Teach character without your child even knowing they are being taught. Everyday examples set by good parenting isn't found in a textbook. They are learned over time. Take the time. Don't allow your child to be a statistic.

Did you tell your kids you love them today?

October 4

FEAST OF ST. FRANCIS OF ASSISI

So, you think you have given up some things in your life? It is said that St. Francis gave up everything. Literally. He rejected everything his father gave him, even his clothes. He stripped down, handed his clothes to his father and walked out of the gates of Assisi to answer God's call to "rebuild my church." He gave up everything to be free to encounter Christ without distraction. His pious efforts attracted followers and he formed a new order of servants called Franciscans. You most certainly have met some Franciscans in your life. What is your call to serve? If you have heard it, have you responded? You probably won't be called to rebuild His church. You won't have to strip down and reject or disown your father. Are you listening? What is your call to serve? What do you need to get rid of to encounter Christ?

Say a prayer today for one of the blessings in your life.

October 5

YOU HAVE A FATHER WHO LOVES YOU

Not everyone has the same experience with a father in their life. Start off by being a father to your children. If you don't have a role model to follow, look up. You have a Father who loves you. For many of you, that will be the only model you need. After all, He gave the world His only Son. Then follow His lead and be the best father you can be to your children. They will know they are loved and you will be forever blessed.

Say a prayer today for one of the blessings in your life.

October 6

MORE THAN A SPERM DONOR

Any man can be a sperm donor. Not all can be a dad. I take that back, everyone who is a sperm donor is a potential dad. It's just that some refuse to take the job. They say it is too hard. "It took away my freedom." I can tell you...they are wrong. Need proof? Take time to play catch with your son. Push your daughter on a swing. Hear her laugh and say, "higher, daddy, higher." Walk with your child barefoot through a babbling brook. You don't have to say anything. Now tell me you don't feel free.

Did you tell your kids you love them today?

October 7

IS IT YOU?

Are you being challenged because of something you said? Did you say it in haste or did you have time to think it through? Be sure to look at yourself in the mirror when you have offended someone by the words you use. If one person is offended, it may be you. If two people are offended it is definitely you. If three people are offended, then you have work to do. Words can offend. When your words offend, apologize. Don't let harsh words linger. Repair the damage before it turns into something unmanageable.

Did you call or text a friend today a message of love?

October 8

57 CHANNELS AND NOTHING ON

Bruce Springsteen was right oh so many years ago. Although, even he could not imagine the exponential growth of not only TV channels, but You Tube and podcasts. Even Bob Hope was quoted as saying TV is a vast wasteland. Don't watch garbage TV. Don't surf from channel to channel, to YouTube after YouTube. Even when your kids aren't watching with you, don't watch garbage TV. They will know what you watch by what you talk about. Be sure you are watching and talking about productions that don't offend your conscience. Help your children make the same decisions.

Did you tell your kids you love them today?

October 9

DADS WITH GIRLS

You are not allowed to say NO. If your daughter wants to play school, or have tea with you, you cannot say NO. When they get older and you are asked and expected to say YES, don't say no to a father daughter dance. These opportunities will sometimes seem like they occur too often. Remember, the opportunities will soon pass away. All girls want a relationship with their fathers. If they don't have that as a memory, their life choices as they apply to relationships with men will forever be a challenge. Be the memory they need. Give the love they need in their formative years. Then, your daughter's life will forever be full of love and memories as well.

Did you tell your kids you love them today?

October 10

BOBBY BOWDEN

Depending on your age and if you watch college football, you may know the name of Bobby Bowden. If you don't, look it up. He was one of the most successful college coaches of all time. Sure, you may have heard stories about him, but did you know this one. Shortly after he retired, he appeared on the Dan Patrick radio show. During the interview he said, "I have coached thousands of young men over the years and I have seen too many of these young men after their football days are over, get lost and never find their way. Many go back to environments that are unacceptable. Very few have a stable relationship and most do not have a father living with them." He ended by saying, "I'm dedicating the rest of my life to changing that." In his book he shared the following: "Roughly 75% of the young men I coached did not have fathers in their lives. I shared scripture with them because no man in their lives ever had." We need more Bobby Bowdens. We need hundreds, nay, thousands of Bobby Bowdens. Won't you be one?

Whose day did you "make" today?

October 11

BE A FATHER

You are a husband. Maybe you either are or plan to be a father someday. You don't have to be nationally famous. Be "around your house famous." First of all, it will take a burden off the Bobby Bowdens of the world. Secondly, you will be fulfilling your primary role as a father. Be famous within your family for telling corny jokes. Be famous for having bad dance moves. Be famous for listening to old music. Be famous for telling your wife and children you love them. Over time, becoming famous within your family will make you infamous with other families who your wife or kids told them about. Better than being known for not being around at all.

Did you tell your kids you love them today?

October 12

SUCCESS DOESN'T COME EASILY

Are their people in your life that you feel "have it made?" How do you think they got there? Sure, there maybe a few "born with a silver spoon" people in your life. But, aside from them, people have to work for what they have. And once they achieve success, they work to keep that status. Watch out what you call success. Having a loving wife and children you are proud of takes lots of work. You have to sacrifice your time and effort to ensure your family is protected. Success at work or in your family doesn't come easily. But it is worth every second you invest in it. Invest wisely.

Did you tell your wife you love her today?

October 13

BE SILLY

Let your guard down. Be silly with your kids. Share jokes with them. Dance with them. Make funny faces with them. Family pictures are not all meant to be family portraits. Chase them around the house. Let them make pancakes with you in shapes and colors. Who cares if they miss and some of the batter ends up on the floor. You are creating memories. Memories are mental pictures in your children's hearts. Those pictures may not end up on your walls but they are forever etched in their memory. And they will not fade as long as you continue to create new ones. There is so much pain and suffering in the world. Be silly, it doesn't cost a thing.

Did you tell your kids you love them today?

October 14

LATE NIGHT DRIVER

As your children got older, you were probably asked to either take them and a few friends to a game or a dance or to a friend's house. (Those of you whose children are not yet at this age, listen.) Many times, their plans fell through because there were plenty of dads who would drive to the event, but very few who wanted to be the late night driver. Do you wish now that maybe you had said "Yes" more often? Sure, you'd had a long day and used that as an excuse. It seems like a simple thing to have said. Then, your children were grown up and out of your home too soon. You don't get second chances to build lasting relationships. (Do you young guys get the message?) Tell them "yes." Wake up from your evening nap and be the late-night driver. There's plenty of time for naps when you are old.

Did you tell your kids you love them today?

October 15

DON'T BE "THAT DAD"

If your children are involved in sports, let your children compete knowing you are there to support them, not live out your own personal dreams. Very few of us set out to be "that dad," but in our desire for the best for our children, we can get carried away. Even though you may think you know better than the coach, keep your mouth shut. You will rarely help a situation by confronting a coach. Even if they are wrong your confronting them will only make things worse for your child. Coaches are paid very little, if at all, for their time. Be nothing but supportive for your child during the season. After the season is over, ask the coach if you could have a conversation with them. Especially if your child will be playing the same sport next year. Be calm. Be supportive. Don't be "that dad."

Did you tell your kids you love them today?

October 16

MOM AND DAD, LEARN TO SAY NO

Have we forgotten how to say, "NO?" Authority matters. Your authority matters. Taking charge in your household in a loving manner will be a valuable lesson to your children. They will be surrounded by children whose parents don't say no and remind you of that. Don't use the line: "Well if you like it at their house, why not go live there." That will only backfire. Say "NO" when you mean "NO." Children have to learn to accept what no means. If not taught correctly, this will only come to haunt them later in life. Just wait. They will eventually thank you for teaching them to accept and understand "NO." Then watch them have the same trials with their own children. It will bring a smile to their face and yours.

Did you tell your kids you love them today?

October 17

BE THE VISIBLE MINORITY

You as a father are fighting an uphill battle. Statistics show that less than fifty percent of children in America live with their biological father. So, what is the battle? To change the percentages in children's favor. You will receive backlash from those who say it is a moral issue that offends children who don't have a father if you try to address "the elephant in the room." Guess what? The elephant needs to go on a diet. Families will get stronger. Children will be more confident. Ultimately our country will be stronger. Fight for what was proven to work for centuries. Kids need a mother and father living in their home. Be part of the visible minority. Fight for your right to defend the family at every turn.

Did you tell your kids you love them today?

October 18

IT'S A LOT EASIER TO REMEMBER THE TRUTH

It's a lot easier to remember the truth. Don't believe me? Think back to times in the past when either you or a loved one or a co-worker was caught in a lie. How did that work out for them? It can take months, years or in some cases a lifetime to live down a lie. The reverse is also true. Telling the truth may cost you a little in the short term, but you, those you love and those you work with will not have to be burdened with the long-term effects of a lie.

Say a prayer today for one of the blessings in your life.

October 19

UNINTENDED CONSEQUENCES

The Information Age has morphed into the Disinformation Age. Some founders and leaders of the largest social media sites don't allow their children to have cell phones. Imagine that? What these men and women created, for the rest of the world to hook into, is acknowledged by the very people who created them to be harmful. Don't believe me? If you watch "The Social Dilemma" you will have more than enough reason to be afraid. Did these men and women set out to create the problems we are now facing? Let's hope not. But follow their own advice and limit your family's exposure to social media. Don't be caught in the unintended consequences of too much media exposure.

Did you tell your kids you love them today?

October 20

RECOVER FROM YOUR MISTAKES

The axiom that "what does not kill you makes you stronger" is never more true than when it comes to parenting. There is no handbook that list the rules of parenting. If you didn't get it from your parents, it becomes "on the job training." Face it, you will make mistakes. Just don't make big ones. Resist temptations to cheat on your wife. Never lie to her. Don't use staying late at work as an excuse to avoid family responsibilities. When you screw up, admit it. Apologize to your wife. If your children were affected by a mistake, tell them you love them and will try to not repeat your actions. You will make mistakes. Don't make the same mistake twice.

Whose day did you "make" today?

October 21

BLOW OFF STEAM SOMEWHERE PRIVATE

Something is boiling up inside of you. You cannot pinpoint it, but you are ready to let someone have it. Don't take it out on someone at home. It wasn't your wife or your kid's that started the issue in the first place. But your inclination will be to take it out on someone you love, just because they are around. Squelch the impulse. If you own a dog, grab its leash and take it for a walk. Go for a run. Go for a drive. Blow off the steam in private. Then return refreshed. Everyone, including you, will be better for it.

Say a prayer today for one of the blessings in your life.

October 22

SLEEP THE SLEEP OF THE JUST

If you are not in the habit of doing so, tonight when you put your head on your pillow, settle in and ask: "How did I do today?" If you receive an immediate positive answer, you will fall asleep much easier. If the answer is somewhat fuzzy, take a moment to reflect on your day. Think about what you could have done better. Don't be hard on yourself, just make yourself aware of what it was that may keep you awake tonight. If you have four or five nights in a row where the answer is still fuzzy, then you have some work to do. Tomorrow when you wake up, think about the day ahead. What could throw your plans off? Where do I need to be extra aware of how I am going to treat or be perceived by others? Then, put it in God's hands. Ask Him to guide you. That way, when you lay your head on your pillow tonight, you will have a positive answer to your question: "How did I do today?" Then, enjoy the "sleep of the just." You earned it.

Say a prayer today for one of the blessings in your life.

October 23

YOU CAN MAKE TIME STOP

Did ever think you could make time stop? Then one day you find yourself laughing so hard with your children that you can barely breathe. Or, maybe you are lying in bed with your wife, holding each other tight in your arms because of the realization of great joy. Or, you are holding each other just as tight due to great sorrow. So tight that nothing else can invade your senses. You are sharing a moment of carefree timelessness. Seemingly you have never felt more alive. Maybe it's because you actually haven't ever felt more alive. In moments like these, don't forget to give thanks to the One who makes it all possible.

Say a prayer today for one of the blessings in your life.

October 24

BE A FAN, NOT A FANATIC

Having a favorite team, or rock band or hobby is a good thing unless it is taken to the extreme. Do you find yourself talking about your favorite team day after day, week after week to the extent that those around you turn a deaf ear? Do you listen to and attend concert after concert of the same artist? If you go fishing or golfing (you pick the hobby) literally every chance you get, you have become a fanatic. Family life and fanatic life rarely go together well. Be sure that your fandom doesn't neglect your role as husband, father and friend. Or soon, you could be rooting all alone.

Did you tell your wife you love her today?

October 25

KNOW WHAT YOU DON'T KNOW

We have all been around guys that "know it all." You find yourself looking for reasons to excuse yourself from his presence. Don't be one of those guys. Know what you don't know. It is amazing what you can learn by keeping your mouth shut.

Did you call or text a friend a message of hope today?

October 26

MENTAL STRESS

Aside from the lack of fathers in over fifty percent of the families in America, the lack of moral teaching in our schools, and in what children see on social media, it is little wonder that the increase in the use of porn, illicit drugs, and sexual promiscuity has led to an alarming increase in mental illness from high schoolers down to primary grades. When children are not taught proper parameters, and/or when they don't have the positive influence of a loving father in their home, they are left to themselves to make decisions that can affect their lives forever. Does this sound like preaching? Yes it is. But it is what is lacking in an alarming number of children's lives. Be aware of the signs of mental stress on your children. Don't be afraid to reach out for help if you have any inkling of mental stress. Act now, before it is too late.

Did you tell your kids you love them today?

October 27

DO IT TOGETHER

As your family grows older and your children get married and have their own children, plan a vacation together once in a while. Don't expect it to happen yearly, although in some families it may. It doesn't have to be a full week. A weekend camping or visiting a national park may be all you find time for, but do it. The planning of the trip can be just as much fun as the trip itself. Let your kids take turns suggesting the location. The memories you will create will last beyond your and their lifetimes.

Did you tell your kids you love them today?

October 28

HOW DO YOU EVANGELIZE

Let me guess. When you go to Church on Sunday you probably sit in the same pew or general area of the Church. Most of us do. Do you know who is sitting next to you? Or behind you? Each of us is called to Evangelize. What better way to do that than to introduce yourself to a fellow parishioner. It isn't difficult. In fact, maybe by you introducing yourself, you may "break the ice" and others around you will follow your lead. Then maybe next week, the guy sitting behind you will introduce himself to the person behind him and before you know it, you are all friends. My guess is, that is the way He planned it.

Whose day did you "make" today?

October 29

HOW MANY PALL BEARERS?

If you died today, how many pall bearers would step up for you? Put aside the morbid thought of death and simply ponder those around you. Can you name two, three, five or more people who walk with you through life? Don't worry, you are not alone if yours is a short list. The good thing is, you have time to work on and add a few to your list. How do you make the list longer? Be a friend. Become someone that someone else would want you to be one of their pall bearers. You've got time.

Say a prayer today for one of the blessings in your life.

October 30

COOLING OFF PERIOD

Face it, our emotions can get in the way. Depending on how long you have been married, disagreements are bound to occur. Petty disagreements have a way of solving themselves. From time to time, you will be faced with situations that present a roadblock between you and your wife. You will be presented with a choice. Either you will want to have immediate resolution to the situation or you will allow for a cooling off period. Choose the latter. You may find it helpful to confide in a close friend or relative. If after a cooling off period of 24 to 48 hours the situation is still volatile, attempt to discuss it with your wife. Each of you should consider listening to each other before expecting the result you wanted. Know that being human, we will not always receive the answer we wanted or expected. Be open to each other and understand that there may just be some issues that the two of you don't agree on.

Did you call or text a friend a message of hope today?

October 31

FAVORITE FOODS... IN MODERATION

Just about every man is known for something he enjoys eating above anything else. A thick steak. Barbeque ribs. A big bowl of ice cream. Chips and salsa, with hot peppers. Hot brownies or chocolate chip cookies. We all have our favorites and weaknesses. It's okay to be known for your favorite. Just don't be known for too much of your favorite. "Everything in moderation, grasshopper."

Did you call or text a friend a message of hope today?

“He has distributed freely, He has given to the poor.”

– PSALM 112:9

November 1

SEEK OUT A MENTOR

If you find yourself on an island when your relationship with your wife and/or children gets off course, find someone to help you get through tough times. Find someone who will challenge you. It may be a co-worker, a pastor, a golf buddy, maybe your neighbor. Don't go it alone. Sometimes just spelling out to someone who will listen will be all the medicine you need. Hearing yourself spew out your troubles can provide clarity. You will have better luck sharing your challenges with someone, than trying to hold it all inside. You are not the first person who needed to seek help. Look for a mentor. The solution may not be as far away as it seems.

Say a prayer today for one of the blessings in your life.

November 2

YOU ARE RESPONSIBLE FOR THE LIFE YOU LIVE

Each of us is ultimately responsible for the life we live. This ultimate responsibility is not judged by man. Although, it is admired by those who also accept responsibility. It is only in the final judgement that our actions are brought to light. Will your actions save or doom you? If we live The Kingdom of God on earth, His judgement saves us. It is your choice.

Whose day did you "make" today?

November 3
NO SUCH STATISTIC

There is no stat that you can find that supports the lack of a father in the home. Go ahead and look. Along the way, you will find countless statistics that show the negative side of a child not having a father in their life. And yet, the government and social service agencies do little or nothing to support an intact family unit. Fathers must fend for themselves to find attention for what they bring to the family unit. Do everything you can to not be a negative statistic. It will be a positive for your children and your wife. It may even help turn the statistics around for those who see what an intact family unit looks like.

Did you tell your kids you love them today?

November 4

DON'T MISS IT (ROUND TWO)

Celebrating victories or academic success with your children is important. But it is equally important to be there when they fail. A dropped pass on the goal line. A soccer kick that hit the post. A forgotten line in a school play. A fall during a dance routine. Your child will soon forget what happened if you are there to hug them afterward. Young kids can be easily soothed with ice cream or a bag of chips. The older they get, the more consolation they need. Don't miss the failures or the victories. They need you there in either case.

Did you tell your kids you love them today?

November 5

YOU ARE NOT ALONE

In the fifties and sixties, all TV families were one big happy family. Yea, like that was reality. Truth be told, even in what you would call the "best" families there are things going on that you will never know about. So, when tough times hit you, know that you are not alone. What will define you is how you get through the tough times. Make sure its not at the bottom of your second, third or fourth can of beer. That will only lead to more trouble. Face it head on. Walk hand in hand with your wife. Or, call a brother or other family member to share what's going on. They may not have the answer you are looking for. But simply talking with someone will get you halfway to the answer, which is closer than you were before you started.

Did you tell your wife you love her today?

November 6

A GOOD NIGHT'S SLEEP

Experts agree that a healthy lifestyle must include a good night's sleep. Yet, we neglect to give ourselves this elusive goal. Look around you. Who do you know that seems the most fulfilled? The most energetic? The most productive? I bet if you ask them, one of the things they will have in common is a regular sleep schedule. It may be just six and a half or seven hours, maybe even eight hours. But it will be regular. Look at your sleep schedule. If it is erratic, work towards making it more regular. You will soon notice a difference. Those around you will begin to notice the difference as well. It's a gift. Open it.

Say a prayer today for one of the blessings in your life.

November 7

FROM SMALL THINGS, BIG THINGS SOMEDAY COME

Strive for little victories. Make sure your kids know you are proud of them when they discover something new or think of a fun way to do something. Praise them for polite behavior. Praise them for straightening up their room. Small things matter. Doing small things well will lead to doing bigger things down the road. Plant the seeds of success without them even realizing it. Then watch them bloom.

Did you tell your kids you love them today?

November 8

YOUR CHILDREN'S FREE SPIRITS

It was said many years ago that "Your children come through you, they are not of you." Despite your best efforts and all the love you can possibly give, some children may reject their parents. It happens even in the best homes. You have no control over a child that just doesn't see eye-to-eye with you. It's not your fault. In many cases, all you can do is pray. Children can tear your heart out. It could be life just longing for itself. It could be mental. Love them anyway. Make sure they know that they are welcome back home. Some will return, some may not. Of course, you will feel guilty and blame yourself. Give it up to God. He will sort it out. Do your best. That's all God asks of you.

Did you tell your kids you love them today?

November 9
PRECIOUS TIME LEFT

How old are your children? Regardless of their age, they are another day older today. One day closer to being "grown up and out of the house." They will be gone in the blink of an eye. It will happen a lot sooner than you think. What more reason do you need to say yes to them when they want to play with you? Or ask you to read to them. Or play a game with them. Do your best to say yes to their request, regardless of how tired you may be. They will remember a lot more about the day-to-day presence you were in their lives as they get older. Give them lots of memories. They will become treasures of your own as well.

Did you tell your kids you love them today?

November 10

BUILD UP RATHER THAN TEAR DOWN

Taking a stand for the truth is not as easy as we think. In trying to defend our actions, sometimes we try to tear down our alleged opponent, rather than admit where the truth actually lies. Often, we can paint ourselves into a corner with no way out. When confronted with defending a thought or action, if you find yourself tearing someone else down instead of building them up, chances are you have taken the wrong stance. Building each other up is rarely the wrong stance.

Whose day did you "make" today?

November 11

THANK A VETERAN

In our day, veterans have been given little notice for their service. The past two generations still blame veterans for the decisions of those in political office in the sixties and seventies that perpetuated a war that should not have drug on and on. The decisions surrounding the Vietnam War effort fall squarely on politicians who lied to the American people. Over time, we have finally begun to give veterans of all wars their proper respect. If you run into a vet from any war, thank them for their service. World War II vets on down through those who fought in the Gulf War and Afghanistan. Thank and respect those who fought for our ability to live in a country free of tyranny. And pray that there are fewer wars to fight in the years to come.

Say a prayer today for one of the blessings in your life.

November 12

WE ARE NOT EXTINCT

As time passes, the role of fathers keeps being pushed aside as a thing of the past. As an attempt by many to reduce the so-called male dominated society, fatherhood is rarely emphasized as a benefit to society. Fathers are looked at as dinosaurs. Despite the best efforts of those who would like you to believe this to be true, although fathers may be looked at as dinosaurs, we are not extinct. At some point, in I hope the not to distant future, fathers will once again be looked at with the respect that mothers have held all along. Granted, many men have abdicated their roles as fathers, shedding a dark shadow on those of us who remain. But society needs both strong mothers and fathers to provide the backbone of society. Biologically, without fathers, the entire world would be extinct. Socially, the same truth exists.

Did you tell your kids you love them today?

November 13

STORMS WILL COME

There are few people who have ever lived that did not have to face storms in their lives. In fact, you could probably state that it may never have happened. Storms will come. It is how you weather the storms that determines your success. It seems that the best remedy for facing storms is to face them together. Few storms are defeated alone. The rise of the incidence of mental health struggles demands that we band together to help each other through the storms we all face. Recognize when those around you are struggling. You may not have the answer to help quiet the storm, so help them find someone(s) who can. Any fight is made easier when we weather the storm together.

Did you call or text a friend a message of hope today?

November 14

IT'S BEEN A LONG DAY

You came home two hours late because the project you were working on blew up. Or your wife got caught in traffic. Or there were three places the kids needed to be tonight and you haven't said one word to each other since last night. You sink into bed, just wanting a moment of peace. Don't let the day be totally lost. Even if she has been in bed for over an hour as you try to wind down, roll over and hold her in your arms. You may not even need words. But that connection will be just enough to make the day worth it after all.

Did you tell your wife you love her today?

November 15

GIVE THANKS

When was the last time you gave thanks to God for your wife? Did you tell her you love her today? We can find ourselves getting so caught up in the day-to-day happenings in our lives that we forget to acknowledge those we love most. Aside from thanking God for each new day, we need to give thanks for our spouse as well. Even on days that have not gone the way you want, be sure to tell your wife that you love her before you go to bed each night. Remember when you were dating and everything seemed new and you wanted so much for each other. Start each new day with that same thought. It will bring endless joy to your day...and hers.

Did you tell your wife you love her today?

November 16

KNOW YOUR LIMIT

Finding yourself stretched too thin? Are you trying to be too many things to too many people? In attempting to be noticed, loved, appreciated, etc., you may become spread so thin that just the opposite becomes the reality. Use the following as your guide: Have you neglected the needs of your wife? Have you neglected the needs of your children? Is your work suffering? Are you tired all the time? Positive answers to one, two or three of these questions will provide the answer you need. Don't spread yourself so thin that you are of no good to anyone. Know your limit.

Say a prayer today for one of the blessings in your life.

November 17

NO ONE TO SHARE IT WITH

You probably have seen it happen. Your relative or a co-worker gets so intent on being "successful" that he forgets what's important. He gets caught doing more than flirting. Usually after it is too late. He ends up with visiting rights on weekends and a one-bedroom apartment. Success is nothing if you don't have anyone to share it with. Keep life in perspective. Money is great. Success at great. But watch the price you pay along the way. You may end up with no one to share it with.

Did you tell your wife you love her today?

November 18

I WANT TO HEAR MY VOICE

My favorite radio voice of all time used to write bits about fake news conferences and there was always the cacophony of reporters shouting: "I want to hear my voice, I want to hear my voice." The joke was that it wasn't what they were reporting that was important, it was simply that they were heard. When you have an opportunity to speak, think less about being heard and more about what you are to say. You may not always have your voice heard. But what you say will be remembered.

Whose day did you "make" today?

November 19

IF ONLY I HAD A MILLION BUCKS!

Have you ever really thought about becoming an instant millionaire? One day you are living a "work-a-day" job and the next day, heck you could retire. Then what would you do? There are countless stories of mega-million winners who in just a few years have spent their winnings and are actually in debt. Count your blessings. If you think about it, your happiness has little to do with money and more to do with who you are sharing your life with. Share what you have. Share love freely. You will spend less time worrying about what you don't have.

Say a prayer today for one of the blessings in your life.

November 20
WHO GETS TO HEAVEN?

There is no shortcut to heaven. It has to be earned. Of course, the saints are in heaven: Mother Teresa, St. Francis. Everybody's deceased grandma is in heaven.:) Deciding to work for eternal salvation is a lifelong job. Do the work necessary to gain entrance to the eternal kingdom. Word has it that your constant work toward salvation is infinitely worth it in the long run. Do the work. Gain the reward.

Say a prayer today for one of the blessings in your life.

November 21

LET IT BE

Your wife lost her keys, again. Or she left the lights on inside her car. Or she...for the umpteenth time. Get over it. You are not perfect either. Sure, you want to point out her repeated foibles. Let it be. There are bigger fish to fry. Wake up fresh tomorrow. Chances are you will already have forgotten what it was that happened yesterday. Let it be.

Did you tell your wife you love her today?

November 22

ARE YOUR PARENTS AND OR GRANDPARENTS STILL AMONG US?

Just as you must respect your wife, your parents and grandparents deserve the same respect. Be sure that your parents and grandparents are a vital part of your children's lives. (Sadly, there are some among us that for very valid reasons may not want their children exposed to their parents. Make sure you have very solid reasons for this divide. Be sure that your children know and understand why there is this divide.) Otherwise, take advantage of the love that your parents and grandparents will shower on your children. Your children will know more about love and the tales of past generations that they will pass on to their children. There is no greater gift that you can share.

Did you tell your kids you love them today?

November 23

BE THANKFUL FOR WHAT YOU HAVE

Keeping up with the Jones' is an old saying but one that leads many of us to aspire to a lifestyle that can be beyond our means. Sure, you want a little luxury in your life. But at what price does that come? Many of the Jones' are saddled with debt that turns their life into a constant struggle with financial burdens. Next time you have an inkling to "keep up," first be thankful for what you have. Will buying that new car, or new sofa or remodeling your kitchen strap you with debt that will limit your ability to enjoy life? Be thankful for what you have. Maybe the Jones' wish they were more like you. Did you ever think of that?

Say a prayer today for one of the blessings in your life.

November 24
GAME NIGHT

On the rare occasions when you have their attention, start a regular game night. Kids love games. Once in a while, let them pick the game they want to play. You will have to compromise amongst siblings. If your wife needs some alone time, play games that allow you time with your children. You will be amazed at the conversations that will take place when you are sitting around a game table in friendly competition. They will tell you about their day. They may even ask how your day went. What a great chance to bond without them even knowing what is going on.

Did you tell your kids you love them today?

November 25

THANKSGIVING DAY LORE

I don't think it is just select families who share stories around the annual Thanksgiving dinner celebration. Gatherings with family typically lead to the sharing of stories from the past. For some reason, Thanksgiving stories are the best. The stories are typically not about holidays. They are memories of personal moments that take on greater meaning as time goes by. Or they are stories that could not be told when they occurred because of their nefarious nature. We are not talking about criminal activity. But they may be stories of daring activity where no one got hurt. Every family has these stories. Be sure they are shared. Then watch the legends grow from year to year.

Did you tell your wife you love her today?

November 26

STILL HAVEN'T FOUND WHAT YOU ARE LOOKING FOR?

Young or old, we are always searching. Some searches take more time than others. Some searches may indeed take a lifetime. What are you looking for? Does anyone else know what you are looking for? You may find that it is much easier to find what you are looking for if others help along the way. You see, they are searching also. Share what you are looking for and your search may be a lot shorter than you'd expect.

Whose day did you "make" today?

November 27

DAILY TIME WITH YOUR WIFE

Face it, we are all too busy. Life has a way of throwing curveballs your way on a daily basis. Plans can be shot by 8 a.m. Whatever happens on a daily basis, be sure to include a moment or two with your wife. It may not sound like very much, but sometimes, a few moments are all you will have. Having little time with your wife doesn't mean you don't love her. In fact, just the opposite could be true. You or she may have to run the kids here or there. You may have to stay late at work. She may be volunteering somewhere. Life happens. Just be sure that your marriage "happens" on a daily basis. A few moments may be all you get. Cherish them.

Did you tell your wife you love her today?

November 28

AT HOME DINNER FOR TWO

Dinner for two doesn't have to be scheduled at a nice restaurant. You and your wife can have an equally pleasant and much less expensive dinner at home. The two of you can work on the menu. You may want to try to prepare something that is new to both of you to add some additional fun to the evening. Get dressed up. Set the table like guests were coming over. Light a candle or two. Put on your favorite music and simply enjoy each other's company. There is no timetable. And you don't have to leave a tip.

Did you tell your wife you love her today?

November 29

NO ANGRY BED

It's an old saying: "Don't go to bed angry." To anyone who has been married any length of time, this is not always easy. If it is happening a lot, you may need some counseling. If it has only happened infrequently then you should be able to work it out yourselves. Typically, it can be the result of a bad day that one of you had that is brought home. Or a pet peeve is tweaked too many times. Recognize the root of the problem and you are halfway home. Admit you may have just needed someone to bear the brunt of your bad day. You may not end with a hug. Maybe by reaching across, under the covers with one foot, just to make a connection can ease the situation and bring a smile. What do you have to lose by trying?

Did you tell your wife you love her today?

November 30

THE GREATEST STORY EVER TOLD

It has been said that the Bible is the greatest story ever told. What is the story of the Bible? God's undying love for his creation. Can you create a great story in your life? In many ways, you don't get to decide that. It is received and shared by those you love. Every day you have a chance to add to the story of your life. You are the author. Your creation: your marriage and the children you bring into the world, are your greatest story. Give them stories to tell that they will want to share. You will be a great author by becoming and creating their greatest story.

Did you tell your kids you love them today?

"No man is a failure who has friends."

– FROM "IT'S A WONDERFUL LIFE"

December 1

MAKE CHRISTMAS MEMORIES

Christmas is 25 days away. It will be here and gone before you know it. Make plans today to make it special. Your wife and children should be your first priority. But don't forget your parents, family and friends. See, you have more to do than you thought. Start planning today. Make a list for yourself and check off what you complete each day. Celebrate Christmas through the entire season. Not just one day. That will be a gift for you.

Did you tell your kids you love them today?

December 2

SLOW DOWN DURING DECEMBER

In years past, has it seemed like as soon as Thanksgiving is over, Christmas happens too quickly? Especially if you have children, the season can pass before you know it's over. Find some time to slow down this Christmas season. You can even sit with your wife and decide that on one day each week, you and your family will stay home and enjoy the spirit of the season by simply being together. Maybe you can make some popcorn and watch a Christmas movie. Maybe you can bake some cookies and sing Christmas carols. A game night can bring the family closer. Take time to plan on slowing down this Christmas season. I bet you will find that not all gifts are placed under the tree. Some of them are sitting right next to you as you ponder the reason for the season.

Did you tell your wife you love her today?

December 3
LEAVE THE LIGHT ON

Now that the Christmas season has begun, I would like to suggest a new tradition. Find a light in your home and leave it on through the feast of Epiphany. It could be a light in your front window. It could be a night light that you have used for your children. At our home, we have a light in our creche that we turn on each Thanksgiving weekend and do not turn it off until January 6. It will help you remember the reason for the season. There are many distractions during the Christmas season. Starting this tradition, you will have a constant reminder of the gift of life celebrated on December 25. Leave a light on. Remember why we celebrate.

Say a prayer today for one of the blessings in your life.

December 4

BIRTHDAYS ARE IMPORTANT

You know when you find out birthdays are important? When you forget one. Other than Christmas and Easter, there is no more important day each year than your wife's and your children's birthdays. (For some, a birthday may be more important that Christmas or Easter.) Make a point to plan for and celebrate birthdays. Aside from the gifts and dessert, the simple recognition of the gift each member of your family is to your life is reason for celebration. Forget at your own peril. (Need help remembering? Use the calendar in your phone and place birthdates and anniversary dates in your calendar.)

Did you tell your kids you love them today?

December 5

WHOSE DAY DID YOU MAKE TODAY?

You encountered countless people today. Did anyone you encountered receive a negative or listless reaction? You don't have to be "UP" every day. But on days when you are not at your best, don't ruin someone else's day as a result. Regardless of the day you are having, if someone asks how you are doing, try to bring yourself out of whatever negative vibe you are feeling by honestly sharing how you are feeling. Short, snippy negative words will only help to ruin someone else's day. Then, you may even start to feel better simply by not ruining their day. We all have off days. Suck it up and start fresh tomorrow.

Whose day did you "make" today?

December 6

CHRISTMAS GIFT FOR YOUR WIFE

There are as many ways to celebrate Christmas as there are people to celebrate it. How do you celebrate it with your wife? How will you make this year different? Don't use an old excuse such as: "We do the same things every year". Change it up this year. It doesn't have to be an expensive gift. If you are short on ideas, ask you children or ask your wife's sister(s) what they think she would enjoy. Sometimes it **IS** actually the thought that counts. Take some time to find something new or start a new tradition with her. She is the greatest gift in your life. Let her know that on Christmas morning.

Did you tell your wife you love her today?

December 7
SPEAK UP FOR FATHERHOOD

It seems ridiculous to have to even mention this, but you have a responsibility to stand up for fatherhood. The media supports the notion that masculinity is toxic. I say: "Spread the toxicity!" Masculinity is needed just as much as femininity. It's called the propagation of the species. Celebrate masculinity as much as you celebrate femininity. Men and women need each other. It's basic science. It's basic nature. Celebrate together.

Say a prayer today for one of the blessings in your life.

December 8

BE ON TIME

Time is precious. Your time is precious. Those with whom you meet daily also value their time. Respect the value of their time. BE ON TIME! There are countless quotes from business owners to coaches of all sports, who try to relate to those around them that being on time is important. Jobs have been lost and players on teams have been cut because they failed to show up on time. Set your schedule so that you arrive on time. Here's a tip: Plan to arrive fifteen minutes early. You will never disappoint by being early. Most importantly, teach your children to do the same. Being prompt is a very positive attribute today. Show you care by being on time.

Whose day did you "make" today?

December 9

DON'T BE SCROOGE

One of the most popular Christmas stories is Dickens' "A Christmas Carol." There are easily fifty different versions that you can watch. Regardless of the version you watch, your Christmas will be determined by how you also grow in your knowledge of the needs of others in your life through the Christmas season. Don't wait until Christmas Day. Send a letter to someone you haven't seen in a while. Donate your money and especially your time at a retirement center or homeless shelter. The possibilities are endless. Then, on Christmas Day, the gifts under the tree will seem somewhat less important than the feeling you received by not being a Scrooge.

Did you tell your kids you love them today?

December 10

LOVE

To quote the song: "It is what makes the world go 'round." You encounter people every day that don't have love in their lives. Your first job is to make sure your wife is loved. Then be sure your children are loved. Throw in a call or visit with your parents once in a while and you will be showered with so much love that you may sometimes feel guilty. Wrap yourself in that love. Then, let everyone you encounter on a daily basis know you are loved because of the way you treat them. To someone that has little or no love in their life, it doesn't take much. A smile, a wave, a friendly hello. Asking someone you don't know their name is a great sign of respect and love. You have received the gift. Give it freely.

Did you tell your wife you love her today?

December 11

YOUR SPECIAL GIFT THIS CHRISTMAS SEASON

It is a couple of weeks from Christmas. Go out today and buy a Christmas card for your wife and each of your children. Take time to find one with a message that they will enjoy. Then write a personal note to each of them. If you find you need more space, then type a letter and place it inside the card. Your gift to them this Christmas is to tell them how much they mean to you. You have two weeks to complete the messages. Then, hold on to the cards until Christmas Eve when everyone is sleeping with visions of sugarplums in their heads. Place the cards on the Christmas tree. Then, before you do anything else on Christmas morning, ask them to find their cards and read them. The special gift will be the smiles on their faces from an unexpected gift. You will have received an unexpected gift as well. (Try it, and you will find the "meaning" of the season.)

Did you tell your kids you love them today?

December 12

REACHING OUT DURING THE CHRISTMAS SEASON

What are you doing for others this Christmas? Sure, monetary donations are welcomed. But, how did you reach out to others? It could be as simple as baking cookies for your elderly next-door neighbor and taking them to her and sitting with her. Maybe you could go to your parent's home and help them decorate for the season. There are countless opportunities to give some of your time at a retirement center or homeless shelter. Be sure to include your children in whatever you do, regardless of their age. Make Christmas memories that last not only for you, but for those you share the message with. Saying "Merry Christmas" by giving the gift of...YOU.

Whose day did you "make" today?

December 13

RESPECT YOUR WIFE

You have heard it before in these pages...Respect your wife. There are two main reasons you need to show her respect. First, she deserves it. Your marital bond requires total respect for each other. Secondly, your children need to see that you respect her. If you neglect the respect she deserves, your children will follow suit. Then, they will not respect others in their lives and possibly themselves. If they lose respect for themselves, then your have an even bigger problem. Don't leave one shadow of doubt in your children's minds that you do not respect your wife. Guess what? They will give you unending respect as a result.

Did you tell your wife you love her today?

December 14

KIDS NEED FAMILY DINNERS

"...the more often children have dinner with their parents, the less likely they are to smoke, drink or use drugs and parental engagement fostered around the dinner table is one of the most potent tools to help parents raise healthy, drug-free children." (*Cincinnati Enquirer*, September 27, 2010) It was true in 1955, it was true in 2010 and it is true today. You never know what your kids will say or what they will hear, but it is crucial to their development. Having dinner two or three times a week should be the minimum. Many families struggle for one. Make the effort. Make a commitment to the development of your children. The dividends are priceless.

Did you tell your kids you love them today?

December 15
EXPAND YOUR MIND

Expanding your mind includes so many possibilities. Some men find traveling to new spots around the globe to be fulfilling. That is great if you can afford it and I encourage you to do so. Other men find strenuous exercise to be effective in expanding your life experience. One route available to just about anyone is reading. At the very least, explore that route. Saying you don't get anything out of books simply means you haven't found the right genre. Continue to look until your find books that speak to your inner soul. Share what you have found with others. Most especially, share what you have read with your wife and children. They may not hold the same interests as you. But by sharing what hits home for you, may encourage them to do the same.

Did you tell your kids you love them today?

December 16

YOU FIND OUT WHO YOU ARE

There may be no greater life lesson that dealing with failure. Failure comes in all shapes and sizes. When you are young, simple failures can be blown out of proportion. As a parent you need to help your children understand that losing or not getting what you want is part of life. If this lesson isn't learned at an early age, losing or not getting what you want as an adult may have devastating consequences. You help as a parent by not making a big deal out of small things. Teach your children that they will find out who they are when they don't get what they want. There will be examples all around them of friends and relatives who don't deal well with failure. Help make sure your children deal with success and failure without exaggerated drama. Win or lose.

Did you tell your kids you love them today?

December 17
FRIENDS

Most of us have friends from our childhood, either from grade school, high school or college. How do you define a friendship? They are best defined by thinking about what it would be like not to have friends. In your adult years, you will be lucky to count two or three close friends in your life. Consider yourself lucky. Foster friendships by getting involved in your children's activities. Or get involved in your church or school. Some of your best friends will come from shared time with your children. These relationships happen without you even realizing it. Having adult friends comes in real handy in difficult times. Make a friend. Be a friend.

Did you call or text a friend a message of hope today?

December 18

MESSAGES OF HOPE AND LOVE

Today, surprise someone or multiple someones in your life. Send a message to a brother or sister you haven't heard from in a while. Call a friend and schedule a breakfast or lunch. When you get home tonight take your kids out for an ice cream or treat of their choice. Stop and buy a inexpensive bunch of flowers for your wife and/or daughters. It's not the price but the thought that counts. Everyday signs of hope and love help cement relationships. Just like you want to hear it once in a while, be sure those around you know that they are loved. It doesn't always take a lot of effort, but the thought will linger in the recipient's mind. Who knows, maybe they will send a message of hope and love to someone else. And so on and so on.

Did you call or text a friend a message of hope today?

December 19
YOUR PARENTS

In today's society, parents are at a premium. If your parents were a major part of your life, cherish that gift. So many of those you share this planet with do not know the love of a parent or parents. Give that love back to them. They will grow old and that love will be a bond that is never broken. If you did not have a parent in your life, change the cycle. Be sure in your older years that your children have countless reasons to remember they were loved. Life is too short to be lived apart. Live, love, and create memories for a lifetime.

Say a prayer today for one of the blessings in your life.

December 20

OLD STORIES NEVER DIE

There is not a lasting relationship between two people that doesn't have a story to which both of you can relate. That's what makes your relationship special. Many of these stories revolve around holidays. I know a man who will not eat a White Castle hamburger. His wife loves them. He never takes her to White Castle. But on Christmas Day they always seem to drive past a White Castle, which is the only day they are closed and the husbands says: "I wanted to take you to White Castle today, but they are closed." It happens virtually every year. What is the story you share with your wife? Don't ever let it die.

Did you tell your wife you love her today?

December 21

A TEXT WON'T DO

Our communication as a human race has taken an ugly turn. We think that because we can immediately text someone, we are communicating. Nothing takes the place of real human interaction. Countless studies show us that the more impersonal communication we utilize, the less connected we actually are. It is too easy to hide behind a texted response. I have news for you. Your wife, your children, your co-workers and those you worship with are longing for meaningful human interaction. Put down your phone. Use your God-given talent to be part of the lives of those around you.

Say a prayer today for one of the blessings in your life.

December 22
EXTENDED FAMILY STORIES

The larger your family, or the larger your gatherings are around the holidays, there typically isn't enough room at the main or "big" table. Usually, the children are relegated to a smaller table, sometimes in another room. Remember when you first got the "call up" to the "big" table? Then, the stories you only heard whispered from a distance became real. You were all ears. It took a few years, then you joined in on the conversations as well. Remember those times as you raise your own children. Those stories are what makes your family real. They are what makes celebrating the holiday season something you can't wait for each year. Extend the family stories through the generations. Watch not only the stories grow, but watch your children grow with each passing year.

Did you tell your kids you love them today?

December 23

WHO ARE YOU IN THE STORY?

I am assuming you have seen the move, "It's A Wonderful Life." *(If not, do it before Christmas.)* Make sure your wife and children watch it also. It is easily one of the top ten movies of all-time. What character in the movie best describes you? Depending on how old you are, your answer to this question will change. But that is a good thing because it means you are growing and experiencing life. Whether you are helping someone by lending a hand, or maybe you need someone to lift you up, there is a character for you. You may even see some of the villain in you. That is ok as long as you recognize your faults and need to change. If you are like many people I know, watching it will become a yearly event. A yearly event to see how you have changed since last year. Then ask yourself: "How did you live your wonderful life in the past year?"

Say a prayer today for one of the blessings in your life.

December 24

LIFE'S GREATEST GIFTS: YOUR WIFE

Let's start at the top. Your wife is the greatest gift in your life. There is no argument. Sure, there will be times when you may feel distant from each other, but do your best to make those times as short as possible. How do you do that? Remember the best days with your wife. Keep them top of mind. Share those "bests" with your wife regularly so you both remember why you fell in love in the first place. Build on that. Besides, the best days, if you really think about it, are most days. Don't let less than the best come between you and the one you love most. Cherish the gift.

Did you tell your wife you love her today?

December 25

LIFE'S GREATEST GIFTS: YOUR CHILDREN

Depending on the age of your children, you will sometimes have reasons to question why is it that you love them so much. The single most important reason is the undying love they have for you. How do you ensure that it will last? Give the love back to them. Remember when they were young and they couldn't wait for you and your wife to get home from work. They had to tell you about their day, even when all you wanted to do was sit in peace for a few minutes. As they get older, kids will find other ways to entertain themselves but be sure you are part of it. They will grow up and have lives of their own. Make sure they know what love is by sharing it with them. It's yours to give, don't be frugal.

Did you tell your kids you love them today?

December 26
YOU MADE IT THROUGH ANOTHER CHRISTMAS

What does your home look like this morning? What thoughts are filling your mind? Are you tired because you partied too hard the past few days? Why not start today with a thank you to your wife for the gift she is. You made it through another Christmas. If possible, take the rest of the day to answer this question: "Over the past month, for whom did you help create lasting memories?" Here's hoping you have a list of positive answers.

Say a prayer today for one of the blessings in your life.

December 27
BE AUTHENTIC

There is only one you. Don't spend your life trying to be someone else. You were placed here at this time and in this place to make a difference. Find your authentic self. Don't be afraid to share your authentic self with others. They are struggling to be authentic as well. By showing how you are working to be the best you can be, it may rub off on someone else. Each man and woman on this earth is longing to find meaning in their own lives. Be authentic. Think about it. What else could you truly be?

Whose day did you "make" today?

December 28

YOU CANNOT DRINK A GOOD RED WINE TOO SLOWLY

The best things in life are meant to be enjoyed at a relaxed pace. Binge drinking rarely ends up well. Take life as you would a good glass of red wine or a well-aged scotch. Enjoy each sip. Look around at what you have in your life. Appreciate your friends. Love your wife and children. Treat each day like a good glass of red wine. Slowly and with thanks.

Say a prayer today for one of the blessings in your life.

December 29

WHO DO YOU KNOW THAT IS TRULY HAPPY?

I know a woman that spends each weekday morning preparing the church she attends for daily Mass. Sometimes it takes an hour, sometimes longer. She is grateful to have the opportunity to serve in this way, and she receives no earthly reward for it. But she takes great pride in knowing that the parishioners who attend the Mass have no distractions in practicing their faith. Everything is in place. Everything is clean. She is one of the happiest people I have ever met. No earthly reward? Imagine the eternal reward she has waiting for her.

Whose day did you "make" today?

December 30

A GOOD NAP

There is one thing that gets better with age that you may never have thought of. There are some days when nothing beats a good nap. You may not want to admit it, but stopping for a quick nap can be the best thing that happens to you on a Saturday or Sunday afternoon. Cherish it when it happens. It won't happen as often as you would like, but those around you will notice a difference in you when you wake up. Here's a tip: Your wife could probably use a good nap once in a while as well. Gift each other the time to sneak in a quick nap. You will both be better for it.

Did you tell your wife you love her today?

December 31
AULD LANG SYNE

Whenever I think of singing Auld Lang Syne, I always hope that I am singing it with those I love. What better way to celebrate the old year and welcome a new one. The older you get, the more you appreciate a night spent with family and friends. And what better night than New Years Eve to do that kind of celebrating. If you are reading this on New Years Eve morning, what are your plans for tonight. Who will you be celebrating with? It may be just you and your wife. It may be with some members of your family. It may be with good friends. Ring in the New Year with those you love. Wish them a Happy New Year filled with memories of why you are blessed to celebrate with them.

Did you call or text a friend a message of hope today?

ACKNOWLEDGEMENTS

This book is not possible without the undying love of my wife. What she has taught me about love would fill many more books. My children have provided helpful comments and encouragement as I struggled to complete the text. For the love and support of my father, Mr. Leonard Grote and my mother, Mrs. Barbara Grote, and all the lessons about life that they taught me, I am eternally grateful.

I would like to thank Steve Sullivan for his friendship and guidance. He helped show me the way as we edited the content and worked with Ingram Press. Thanks to Tom Miller for his illustration on the front cover and to John Kitzmiller for his interior illustration.

Special thanks to my high school classmate, Mike Collins, for not only diligently editing the content, but for suggestions on content. Thanks also to Deacon Mark Danis for his expertise and friendly encouragement. Thanks to Kate Malo for her insight and assistance with my marketing efforts.

Lastly, I would like to thank my grammar school and high school teachers who taught me how to "think," not what to think. (There is a world of difference between the two.) Special thanks to Mr. Bill Kennedy, Mr. Bob Sauerbrey and Mr. Vince Halloran, all English teachers at my alma mater, LaSalle High School in Cincinnati.

EPILOGUE

As I have shared the draft of what you are reading or have read, I have been asked where my inspiration has come from. That may be the most difficult of all questions to answer. Truly, there is no one answer. Ultimately, my relationship with Our Lord has opened my eyes and my heart. The people He has placed in my life, who have shared their faith with me, are a continuing influence on what you have read.

Depending on how much of the 365 entries you have read, I hope it is obvious that I place great importance on reading. Expanding our minds, to me, is the greatest gift we give ourselves. And, by osmosis, we may end up expanding the minds of those we encounter. I can talk about books for hours. Of course, The Bible is foremost on the list. Below, is just a partial of books that have shaped my thinking. To list all of the books that have influenced me would be an exhaustive list. Who knows if our paths will ever cross, but I welcome any thoughts you have on the books that have impacted your life. (There is no rhyme or reason to the order of the books on the list.)

The Return of The Prodigal Son, Henri J. M. Nouwen
The Imitation of Christ, Thomas A. Kempis
Mere Christianity, C. S. Lewis
Rescued, Fr. John Ricardo
The Divine Comedy, Dante Alighieri

The Lord, Romano Guardini
The Life of Christ, Bishop Fulton Sheen
Jesus of Nazareth (trilogy), Pope Benedict XVI
The Power of Silence, Robert Cardinal Sarah
Rome Sweet Home, Scott Hahn
How to Destroy Western Civilization, Peter J. Kreeft
Mercy in the City, Kerry Weber
The Rhythm of Life, Matthew Kelly
Eternity in the Midst of Time, Fr. Wilfrid Stinnissen, O.C.D.

Happy reading!

www.ingramcontent.com/pod-product-compliance
Ingram Content Group UK Ltd.
Pitfield, Milton Keynes, MK11 3LW, UK
UKHW041951190726
13854UKWH00005B/1905